Booth 73

*Bloomington Days*
©2006

#4085    $7

# Bloomington Days

## Town and Gown in Middle America

## Blaise Cronin

Bloomington, IN  Milton Keynes, UK

authorHOUSE™

*AuthorHouse™*
*1663 Liberty Drive, Suite 200*
*Bloomington, IN 47403*
*www.authorhouse.com*
*Phone: 1-800-839-8640*

*AuthorHouse™ UK Ltd.*
*500 Avebury Boulevard*
*Central Milton Keynes, MK9 2BE*
*www.authorhouse.co.uk*
*Phone: 08001974150*

*First published by AuthorHouse 8/28/2006*

*ISBN: 1-4259-3249-5 (sc)*

*Library of Congress Control Number: 2006903713*

*Printed in the United States of America*
*Bloomington, Indiana*

*This book is printed on acid-free paper.*

FOR KEN GROS LOUIS

# CONTENTS

# MID-WESTERN MOANS

BLOOMINGTON IS A QUIXOTIC MIX OF small-town life and larger-than-life campus, squirreled away in the flatlands of the mid-West. On the surface it is indistinguishable from all those other academic oases, Ann Arbor, Austin, Chapel Hill, where testosterone and youthful ambition are released in abundance yet mercifully out of parental sight. To the passing eye college towns have much in common; to the passing European eye they seem indistinguishable. I turned a blind eye to Bloomington's understated charms for years; still do when I'm of a mind. This is not a town that struts her stuff or favors gaudy; she's very much an acquired taste, a slow seducer. But she sometimes gets her man. Sometimes the man is a celebrated architect; I. M. Pei designed the university's angular Art Museum, a *Wunderkammer* in the wild.

How many times have you heard the phrase, "There's something about..."? Well, there *is* something about Bloomington, its smugness and parochialism notwithstanding, and this book is about that something. Much of that something is, of course, Indiana University (IU). Bloomington desperately needs IU, and IU wouldn't be IU without Bloomington. And, as I've come to learn, too, there's something very special about Old IU—"Hail to Old IU" is Indiana's official Alma Mater song—something that doggedly resists reductionism and the plow of official histories. Neither a panegyric nor pictorial record will suffice, hence this svelte volume of vignettes.

I could tell you that IU has a much trumpeted music school, but that doesn't explain how a culture of music suffused both campus and town over the decades, creating a set of moods and magical moments—a special sensibility, no less—that Ann Arbor, Austin (*pace* the producers of *Austin City Limits*) and the rest can never hope to match. On campus, clocks chime cheerfully, bells toll on the hour and the carillons ring from on high. I echo the sentiment of Roland Barthes: "For me the noise of Time is not sad."

Bloomington soothes the soul, yet saps the spirit like no other place I know. Here torpor is mistaken for nirvanic serenity. I perk up as I crest into the town back from wherever. Twenty-four hours later and the *ennui* count begins to rise. I once visited West Berlin before the Wall came tumbling down, and I recall vividly the sense of being free to move about yet somehow feeling corralled as if by an invisible dog fence. Bloomington is my West Berlin. I am at once at home, yet naggingly deracinated. I know I can leave, but, really, I can't. I'm in an open prison and, if not exactly *heureux comme Dieu en France*, almost liking life in this liminal zone.

A *New Yorker* profile of George Gershwin described his recurrent epistolary references to loneliness as being "like a blues line moaning under a jaunty melody." Life in Bloomington is just that. These pages—penned at snatched moments over the years—are a self-indulgent attempt to explain why. But it is not really about me, a Brit abroad; it's about Bloomington and Middle America and what makes them what they are; more specifically, it's about the personality and persistence of a rather special university—the gown in the title—one that is much more than the sum of its many fascinating and occasionally infuriating parts; one that on a good day exemplifies the finest traditions of American higher education. And, I should point out in the interests of full disclosure, one that is, as I write, my beneficent employer.

# IS THAT BLOOMINGTON OR BLOOMINGTON?

THERE'S ONLY ONE BLOOMINGTON. IN INDIANA, that is. There are nine others pebble-dashed across the United States. They don't matter, of course, except at the Chicago check-in desk. Not a few first-time visitors have wondered why they're staring at cornfields in Illinois when they should be admiring Indiana's soybeans. How many careers and love lives have been rerouted because someone failed to distinguish IL from IN on a flight departures board? I wondered as much that chill November night in 1985 when I found myself in the dinkiest imaginable airport waiting for *mein* host. The puddle jumper was parked, its pilot long since gone. Not a fellow passenger, not a soul could be seen. I was utterly alone in an airport in Bloomington. But which Bloomington?

Robert Merton, the late, great sociologist, beat me to Bloomington airport by almost a decade. There was a lovely story in the *New York Times* some years ago that described the patrician Merton striding purposively across the Bloomington tarmac to bring the already departing plane to a halt: he had forgotten to offload his bag. The *NYT* journalist used this as an illustration of Merton's

4

tremendous self-confidence—his belief that he could distinguish fact from falsehood, that his interventions could make a difference in professional life. That's journalism for you. Had Merton put down roots in Bloomington he might have wanted to intervene more than would have been good for him. In idyllic Bloomington—"Tree City USA," summer home to the Beaux Arts trio and a town with more unused bicycle lanes than Calcutta has beggars—reality and revery, as we shall see, have a funny habit of blurring.

It's not that Bloomington isn't a nice sort of place; it is, especially, we mutter *sotto voce*, when the 35,000 students are off on their summer vacations. Crime is largely imagined (this, after all is the 25th safest metro area in the entire United States), or experienced vicariously on "Cops." In the local rag, "Three IU students charged in theft from pop machine" warranted five column inches; "Man arrested for blowing mucus from nose at officer" scored four. But there are some troubling signs that reality may finally be closing in on our Edenic existence. We shall see...

Bloomington (population roughly 100,000 with students included; double that if you count the pesky squirrels) is squeaky clean, and, I'm reliably informed, Indiana University, bedizened in local limestone, is one of the prettiest campuses either side of the Appalachians. Jonathan Gathorne-Hardy, British biographer of sometime IU sexologist Alfred Kinsey, whom we'll encounter later, describes the campus buildings as "Charles Adams Gothic or Scotch Baronial or like prisons or nuclear power stations." I got the short straw; mine is more Lubyanka than Royal Balmoral. The people— the academics, that is, the ones with *summa cum laude* degrees from Harvard, Yale and other Ivies—are not just nice, but almost insufferably so. I'm reminded daily of a remark by Terry Eagleton on the climate of contemporary America: "feeling negative becomes a thought-crime, and satire a form of political treason."

But back to Bloomington airport—Monroe County Airport, to give it its full title. Unfortunately, the puddle jumpers that ferried us to the Windy City and thence to other continents no longer jump. The puddles are still there, but the business, oddly, isn't, which means we have to drive to Indianapolis International Airport to catch a flight…to catch another flight. Proposals for a monorail between Bloomington and the state capital remain stalled in the stratosphere of speculation. The intriguing thing about self-important Indianapolis International Airport is that it doesn't get within an ass's roar of the appellation—unless you count an occasional holiday special to Cancun as evidence of extraterritorial service. Indianapolis may pride itself on being the 14th, 16th or whatever biggest city in the United States, but you can't travel to the Old World from it. Indeed, large tracts of the New World are unreachable from the Circle City, as this blandest of modern metropolises likes to be known. All of which serves to reinforce Bloomington's otherworldliness; it is the epicenter of the *Dar-ul-Harb* (domain of the infidels) which is both the good news and the bad news, I suppose.

These travel-related frustrations affect only *hoi polloi* such as myself. If your name is John Mellencamp and you're married to an ex-*Victoria's Secret* model, things will be different; and, no, I'm not referring to the rumored helipad at the rock star's lakeside home outside Bloomington. Mr. Mellencamp, being a man of means, has access to a customized Boeing 727 parked at Bloomington's decidedly non-international airport. This gleaming metal bird is owned by our resident billionaire, whose name has featured regularly on the *Forbes 400* list of the richest people in the U.S.A. There's none of Aldrich's old money in Bloomington, just some moneyed oldsters and a handful of textbook entrepreneurs. Bill Cook—founder of the world's largest privately held manufacturer of medical devices is one such; a charming, smart-as-pins fellow, whose net worth is well beyond the imagination of the average abacus. He once told me about his 727 as if he were describing a Dodge pick-up truck, but still I had trouble imagining two-seater monoplanes and a full-blown commercial airliner sitting cheek by jowl on the (now smoothed and extended) runway of the otherwise still tiny airport where Merton and many other academics began their fleeting flirtations with Tree City.

The phrase "town and gown" could have been coined with Bloomington in mind. It's the Armonk of academia; except here Blue Blue is Big Red. Red and white (cream and crimson, in truth) are the official colors of Indiana University. Big Red and Bloomington, it's a marriage made in heartland heaven. The city's character—as with other collegiate centers of learning and under-age boozing—is shaped by its permanent population of serious scholars (who vote Democrat) and the shifting shoals of students (who vote on *American Idol*). The locals, a coalition of crusty Christian conservatives and stoic minimum-wage earners, seem to get along fairly comfortably with the privileged majority—IU isn't Duke and Bloomington isn't Durham. Townies and Gownies rarely come to blows; there is none of the muted suspicion one still finds today in the venerable city of Oxford even after 800 years of co-existence. Indeed, a former Bloomington mayor saw IU and the city as parts of a whole rather than two separate entities: "We tend to not recognize the town/gown dichotomy, because it suggests a separation between the two." The university for its part takes its community role seriously, having established (what else?) a Town and Gown Committee a decade ago to "develop a dynamic agenda of common challenges." Worthy if narcoleptic stuff.

On campus high brow and low brow become easily entwined: the likes of Mikhail Gorbachev and Willie Nelson, Al Sharpton and Bob Dylan pop up occasionally, drawing all sorts, from celeb spotters to hero worshippers. The Dali Lama, armed to the teeth with honorary doctorates and peace prizes, is a regular. And every so often the university hosts a public forum on the issue of the day (hurricanes, terrorism, racism) at which notable Townies and Gownies hold forth with the requisite admixture of worldly compassion and touching earnestness. Here churches, synagogues and mosques stand together mouthing multicultural mantras. Perhaps Bloomington is a harbinger of Jürgen Habermas's "post-secular society."

Come Monday morning the trash bags are lined up like chocolate soldiers; twigs, soda cans, plastic, paper, refuse. Color-coded. *Alles in Ordnung.* As the Good Book (Corinthians I) says: "Let all things be done decently and in order." It's a taxonomist's dream world. If you've moved from DC or LA, you can buy a street here for the same price as a decent family home in Georgetown or Brentwood. That's the kind of incentive needed to make sane folk (the natives talk about folk the way Bertie Wooster banged on about cads) move to the interior.

Naturally, there are bits of the city the mayor would rather you didn't see, but these can usually be spray-painted and relegated to page seven of the *Herald-Times*. If you want to take a walk on the wild side, Bloomington is probably not the place. The city, like any other, has a soft underbelly, but not one blubbery enough to write home about. We have far too many places of worship; far too many sobersides dabbling in watercolors, running ethnic restaurants, fusing bluegrass and hip-hop, writing organic poetry, practicing ta'i chi, power walking, or grinding coffee beans to create the necessary edge. I'm pretty sure Stanley Fish had Bloomington in mind when he penned *The Unbearable Ugliness of Volvos*, for it is here that awfully nice people drive awfully drab cars more awfully than anywhere else on earth. On a really bad day it can take seven minutes to drive from home to office, but that still does not get us close to the national average: 73 minutes. And yet, you'll hear otherwise intelligent human beings talking about "the traffic." I call it "the Bloomington effect," a clear sign that one has not only overstayed one's welcome but lost sight of reality.

You may loose sight of reality in Bloomington, but you will never loose yourself here. This is a tiny town, with little by way of landmarks. There is a well-maintained square that boasts a stolid courthouse. Then there's Kirkwood Avenue—the *Rive Gauche* of Bloomington—home to a clutch of watering holes favored equally by Townies and Gownies. And that's about it, except for the inevitable strip malls. Social life here is event-driven: a music festival, an arts weekend, or a ball game. Spontaneous social combustion is unheard of. For a good time, head to Target, T. J. Maxx, Borders or the Farmers' Market, where, naturally, you will meet the very same people you meet daily at work and the Y(MCA), weekly at Kroger and church, and monthly at dinner parties and the opera. Here, truly, "No man is an island unto himself." We live in one another's pockets, which is amusing for a while but suffocating after a year or two. If you're into people watching, you're in for something of a rude awakening. Bloomington, to be blunt, does not rock; I've often wandered about the deserted streets wondering if a neutron bomb has gone off. This is no place for neophiliacs.

Welcome to the town that has been my home for fifteen years—a place that officially doesn't exist, cartographically speaking. I've stood in front of wall-sized maps of the world, looking at the colored dots that signify cities with populations of $X$ thousand or more. I think of all the places I have been, of all the places I might have settled. Not only have I chosen one that doesn't appear on any self-respecting map or globe; I've chosen one that has nine homographs.

# WHAT'S IN A (FUNNY) NAME?

"Welcome to the Hoosier state!" It sounded like hosiery. What has hose got to do with Indiana? I was puzzled. But, then, most newcomers to this carbohydrated slice of Middle America are puzzled. And don't the natives just love it! Puzzlement provides an opportunity to unleash the full story behind the would-be onomatopoetic nickname, which is everywhere: on sweatshirts, in sporting chants ("Go, Hoosiers, Go!"), woven into the fabric of stump speeches. There's the Hoosier Lottery, Hoosier National Park, Hoosier Association of Science Teachers, Hoosiers *ad nauseam*. The lead story in today's *Indiana Daily Student* (*IDS*) is "Hoosiers come up short against UNC." Here, people unselfconsciously refer to themselves as Hoosiers. It's plain natural.

I first encountered the term on a flying visit from the U.K. *Hoosiers* is a tearjerker with Gene Hackman in the reformed-drunk-becomes-miracle-working-basketball-coach-in-rural-Indiana role. I remember watching the in-flight movie, but without sound. It seemed the sensible thing to do at the time. Only years later did I make the connection. I've since re-watched Coach Norm Dale and his high school underdogs and dutifully jerked a few tears (no interloper's cultural adaptation is complete without multiple viewings of both *Hoosiers* and the Bloomington bike movie, *Breaking Away*). If nothing else, it helped me understand why basketball is a form of religion in this part of the world. Orange balls, hoops and Hoosiers: the holy trinity of the Heartland.

Tickets for the IU basketball games are like gold dust: there's never an empty seat in the 16,000-capacity Assembly Hall when the Hoosiers are on court—on or off form. The roof is routinely raised as the clock ticks down. Hell-raising was once part of the Hoosier tradition, but the chair-flinging, towel-slapping, tongue-lashing, media-hugging Bobby Knight was finally booted out, to the relief of many Gownies and the distress of most Townies.

Those other big-time sporting Hoosiers, the IU football team, could do with some of the Hackman magic. Since I've been in town they have compiled one of the most impressive losing records in the Big Ten conference. The latest, over-priced, under-performing coach has just been relieved of his duties. Losing is bad enough, but losing when your 52,000-seater stadium is half full is worse than bad. It has less to do with sporting pride than the economics of higher education. This country is wedded to the principle of "success breeds success." That's as true on as off the football field. A winning streak not only fills Memorial Stadium, but it makes major donors even more willing to write checks to their *alma mater*. Experience shows that Alma matters a lot more to her graduates when she's on a winning streak. And, in this case at least, what is good for Gown is good for Town. The more fans that show up for home games, the bigger the boost to the city's economy. It's a win-win situation, except for the inconvenient fact that the footballing Hoosiers seem averse to winning.

Predictably, there is no definitive answer to the oft-asked question, "What is a Hoosier?" Historians, lexicographers, folklorists and others have come up with a variety of explanations. It may have originated with a 19th century contractor named Samuel Hoosier or Hooser...or it may be a bastardization of "Who's ear?" (I'll spare you the derivation of that one)...or it may come from old English dialect, "hoozer" meaning "high hills." I found all of these in a back issue of the IU *Alumni Magazine*. I also, to my embarrassment, found a throwaway remark that I had long since forgotten about. It appears that in 1992 I confessed to the author of this particular piece (the most requested reprint in the magazine's 70-year history) that I believed the word Hoosier conveyed "pride, a powerful sense of community, a lack of pretense, and a sense of the seasons." I must have been, in the words of Henry Peacham in his book, *The Compleat Gentleman*, "shot up with last night's Mushroome."

But other universities and other states have nicknames, too. For every Hoosier in Indiana there's a Buckeye in Ohio. But why engage in speculation? Monikers like Hoosier have long since taken on lives of their own; they are much more than nicknames for college teams. When the "Go, Hoosiers, Go!" cry erupts in Assembly Hall or Memorial Stadium, Gownies and Townies are as one. Hoosierness transcends "them and us-ness." Just how much can be gathered from the tone of this irate Bloomingtonian's letter to the local paper on the team's latest loss of form: "When they step out onto the court, they're not just representing themselves and IU, they're representing all the fans across the state. These players neither understand what that means or deserve to be called an Indiana Hoosier." Ouch!

Hereabouts, we know what the sitting President of Indiana University means when he talks in public about Hoosier values. It's his politically astute, probably also genuine, way of acknowledging

that Indiana folk behave in down-to-earth fashion, mean what they
say and generally go about their affairs in a respectful manner. As I
have learned, artifice and affect are not much admired in these parts;
certainly not on or around the basketball court where thousands of
Hoosier hearts puff with popcorn-propelled pride every time Mike's
men slam the dunk.

# TIT FOR TAT

My capacious cinder-block office overlooks the arboretum. People come here to watch the stream flow softly down to the weeping willow by the seasonally swollen pond and to gaze wistfully across the campus. Sleet or sun, freshmen, faculty, alumni and even the good burghers of Bloomington congregate unwittingly beneath my window. It's a "must-see" spot. No university tour, physical or virtual, is complete without a stop-off at the arboretum. I've watched oriental wedding groups pose for photos, young lovers pet and pant, philosophers muse abstractedly, and sophomores gather for an early summer class. All human life is here. Over the years I'd become *blasé*. Nothing could surprise me any more. Or, so I thought. But one day—spring 1997 or 1998 I think it was—I almost fell off my perch.

A young, bathing costume-clad lady was posing provocatively in, on and around the little waterfall at the arboretum. Telephoto lenses were going where they shouldn't, and the one young lady soon became several young ladies. A phalanx of photographers, a covey of bathing beauties. I was dumbfounded. I called one of my colleagues to confirm that I wasn't hallucinating. We weren't. Days later I discovered that *Playboy* magazine had been on campus (not for the first or last time) to garner visual material for its special college issue. And here's the good news: in the March 1998 issue there were ten representatives from IU, and only one from Purdue (the state's other university that features on *U.S. News & World Report's* national rankings). Historically, the Boilermakers (as engineering-minded Purdue people are known) have blown us off the football field, but not scored where it counts—in the glamour stakes.

*Playboy* must have been back in town recently because some aspiring journalist was sounding off in the *IDS* about the idiocy of removing one's clothes for Hugh Hefner. If that's the worst thing that happens at IU, I won't lose much sleep. Of course, you'd be daft not to think that sex occasionally rears its ugly head on a campus teeming with 35,000 students. There's enough testosterone in these three square miles to propel an unmanned spaceship to Mars...and back. Earlier this year, a performance of *Lysistrata* generated considerable heat across campus because of partial nudity and bawdiness. This is the university that brought you Alfred Kinsey; a place that has the world's second largest collection of pornography (the Vatican, so goes the old chestnut, is home to the biggest); a campus which nonchalantly announces talks with titles such as "Under their skirts: Looking for sex in the Andes" (this one by a candidate for the chair of the department of Gender Studies, as it happens). The *IDS*, I'm pleased to say, came up trumps this time, roundly castigating the prudes, who probably wished that Aristophanes had written an episode of the Mary Tyler Moore Show instead.

The letter column of the *IDS* is an absolute joy, at once semi-literate, illogical, holier-than-thou, sensitive and enlightened: a window into the collective mind, and a reliable register of prevailing values. The same holds for the staff editorials. My favorite so far this semester has to be the sub-heading provoked by the latest, titivating mail-order catalog from *Abercrombie & Fitch*. "Is nudity in advertising kosher?" "Not," I sorely wanted to reply, "unless it has been circumcised." But I thought the better of it.

In no time *Playboy* and Aristophanes had faded into obscurity. The arrival of Shane's World Enterprises brought big-time concupiscence to campus. It was a sub-editor's dream-come-true. "Aftermath of dorm porn plagues IU," harrumphed an early September headline in the *IDS*. Forget about scantily clad females beside a babbling brook. Here we had a commercial company making porn movies featuring IU students. And how did they penetrate IU's dorms? Simple: an unnamed student provided the film crew access to Teter Quad in exchange for oral sex. Who said the age of barter had passed? Here was a story with legs that went half way to heaven. In no time, IU's sexual athletes were the subject of a *Rolling Stone* article, and on the story rolled in the national media. All most infuriating for the campus administration, which was still reeling from Bloomington's unwelcome ranking as the nation's number one party school by *The Princeton Review*. For the record, sales of Shane's World Volume 32, entitled "Campus Invasion," apparently went through the roof. And all this in exchange for fellatio.

So far, the powers that be haven't followed the lead of Father Paolo Ferrini of San Vincenzo in Italy, who asked his bishop to re-bless weddings that had taken place in the local church. According to a BBC news story, the place of worship had been used as a setting for a porn movie. Religious services were suspended until the shocked villagers' church could be purified. Residents of Teter Quad dorm take note! Cleanse your souls before the beadles are on your case.

# CAMPUS CHEER

THE AVERAGE FRAT BOY PROBABLY THINKS Mario Lanza is an Italian sports car. Few if any will have seen or heard of *The Student Prince*. Even fewer will have any idea what "*Gaudeamus igitur, Juvenes dum sumus*" means. The modern Greeks may not know the Latin words, but they still get the message. Booze flows through fraternities and down teenage throats as if Prohibition were just around the corner. Come Thursday evening the dorms of the contemporary American university are transformed into giant saloons. It matters not one iota that Bloomington is, theoretically, a dry campus or that underage drinking is illegal; students drink. And some drink a lot; on campus and off campus.

'Twere ever thus, of course. The infamous town and gown riot of St. Scholastica's Day in 1354 between students of the University of Oxford and the local citizenry, which resulted in death and mayhem, was triggered by inebriated undergraduates expressing loud disapproval at the wine being served in a tavern. Boozing, brawling and brutish initiation rites were well-documented staples of the medieval university across Europe. Nothing much has changed over the centuries, as Hank Nuwer demonstrated starkly in his book, *Wrongs of Passage*. Pledge brothers are as likely to be asked to clean the men's room with a toothbrush as down a bottle of whiskey neat. The growth in alcohol-related hazing has spawned a mini counseling industry to deal with binge drinking and associated activities.

Binge drinking has been defined in the U.S. as having five or more drinks in one sitting, more than once every two weeks. If that's bingeing, then university administrators surely must have better things to worry about. I read somewhere that the Swedes define a binge as the consumption of half a bottle of spirits or two bottles of wine on the same occasion. The Italians think that consuming an average of eight drinks a day is pretty normal stuff, while bingeing in Britain is commonly defined as consuming eleven or more drinks on a single occasion—par for the beginner's course in Russia. In any case, the do-gooders are out in force on America's campuses, determined to save souls and kidneys. Two national organizations on an anti-bingeing mission are BACCHUS (Boosting Alcohol Consciousness Concerning the Health of University Students) and GAMMA (Greeks Advocating Mature Management of Alcohol). The thinking here seems to be that if state laws and university sanctions can't prevent what is often referred to as high-risk drinking, then we should put the emphasis on education and norm shaping. Here's a sample of current thinking from the director of the IU Alcohol-Drug Information Center: "Our goal is to shoot for long term cultural change which we know will take some patience and time. We are finally taking a comprehensive look at the problem. It is not going to be just one program or one policy but rather a bringing together of a variety of individuals that represent different groups." Given that 40% of college kids binge drink, she's got her work cut out.

I doubt it's the reason we hired our current Education School dean, but he is something of an authority on binge drinking, having authored (I know nothing about his swigging skills) way back in 1983 *The BACCHUS Program Guide: A How-to Manual for Alcohol Abuse Prevention on Campus.* Judging by the almost weekly reports of infractions involving the demon drink, including alcohol poisoning, hazing rituals and date rape, it's going to take more than a how-to manual to create alcohol-free frat (and sorority) houses along Third Street and Jordan Avenue where the Daughters of the American Revolution can safely send their progeny.

Organizations such as BACCHUS and GAMMA are well meaning, if a tad naïve. The same can also be said about some of the "alternative" drinking events that occasionally take place on campus. I spotted a headline in the *IDS* a while back that read: "Hit up a kegger with Dean McKaig." Now, the aforementioned McKaig is our Dean of Students and a decent cove; briefly, I thought he was going to let his hair down with the students and become Dick McKeg (geddit?) for an hour or two. Not so. The keg, I quickly learned, would be filled with root beer. That same week the *IDS* ran another alcohol-free story. This time one of the dorms was sponsoring a Casino Night. Martinis, roulette and slinky croupiers I thought to myself. Not so. Punters were provided with "mocktails" while the roulette wheel spun. "Mocktails"—it's enough to make a teetotaler crack a case of Cristal champagne. If this were med school, we'd be talking about the "sterile field" of student life.

Tailgating is to football as drinking is, well, to tailgating. At a recent home game, some IU students felt a need to relieve themselves…behind trees. I know this not because I was lurking behind the trees but because I read it in the letters page of the *IDS*. The letter was written by a disgusted alumna. She was not, bless her heart, disgusted by the peeing students. Beer, post-consumption, has to go somewhere and if the portable lavatories are full, well, then, behind a tree will simply have do. She was disgusted, and here I quote, by the antics of the campus police (we, being a big university, have our own toy police force which has much of the swagger, some of the paraphernalia but, regrettably, little of the common sense of the real thing) who "zoomed in on bicycles or in golf carts, practically tackled some of them, then arrested/ticketed these kids for indecent exposure. They also Breathalyzed (sic) them."

You know, sometimes living in Bloomington is like being in Singapore. Which is probably not what President Herman B Wells would have wanted. This, after all, was the man who during Prohibition took, "a wild ride to French Lick to buy some speak down there one night." It's there in black and white in his affecting autobiography, *Being Lucky*. Three cheers for Hermie!

# GET YOUR ROCKETTES OFF

IN EVERY COUNTRY ON EARTH, FOOTBALL is an eleven-a-side game played with a round ball and a fishing net or two. Except here, where it's platoons of helmeted beefcake chasing after a deformed rugby ball on something called a gridiron. I once attended a "football" game at IU, sat in the President's box—a lofty eyrie replete with major donors and local big wigs—and wished I had brought my opera glasses (and a full hip flask). The game was *coitus interruptus* on repeat play. It lurched, jerked and finally aborted. I aged perceptibly as the day drained before my drooping eyes. Each team seemed to have thirty, forty or more players; and an entire season, I subsequently discovered, consisted of no more than twelve or fourteen games. By way of comparison, football teams in Britain play fifty or sixty matches per season, with far smaller squads; and, I might add, it (soccer) is a physically much more demanding game, one, moreover, that is played without any body armor. Do these fleshy refrigerators realize what a soft sporting life they lead, I wondered that early fall afternoon perched in my V.I.P. nest? In fairness, everyone else in the cavernous stadium seemed to be having a whale of a time. The atmosphere was benign, and there wasn't a football hooligan to be seen or heard. If only it were thus in Europe.

I've also watched IU's other football team; the real one with eleven unpadded players using their feet to kick a spherical object into a decent-sized net. It was very agreeable experience, though the crowd was but a tenth of the size. Here, too, the civility level was astonishing. Two games separated by a common name, I reflected. But both events did have one thing in common: smiling, short-skirted females bouncing up and down, cheering hysterically and waving pom-poms above their heads. I'd never seen anything quite like it; the closest would be the Tiller Girls at the London Palladium or the Rockettes at Radio City.

At the soccer game, the rising and falling pyramids of cheerleaders interfered with my line of sight. I missed at least one goal because of the out-of-sync antics of the irrepressible, post-pubescent gymnasts in front of my bleacher seat (nationwide 25,000 cheerleaders went to hospital in 2003 as a result of injuries received). "Go IU!", "Go Big Red!" and similar, telegraphic exhortations were squawked out at the most inopportune moments with the sincerest form of insincerity. The girls and their male support system (bull-necked boys formed the pyramids' foundations) had their backs to the playing field, so any correspondence between their robotic movements and the ebb and flow of the game was entirely fortuitous. I tried to be charitable, ever mindful of the fact that I was being exposed to a wholesome facet of American life, but, at the same time, I was flummoxed by it all.

It was only when I visited the IU web site that I grasped just how big a deal this cheerleading thing was within the intercollegiate athletics culture. Cheerleading is no two-bit, back-room operation. First off, there's a head coach plus five assistant coaches devoted to this para-sporting malarkey at IU. (That's more than the Brazilian World Cup-winning football team can boast.) The Cream Cheer Squad consists of 22 smiling youngsters, seven of whom are female. All except one appear to be Caucasian. This squad cheers for Football and Men's Basketball. The Crimson Cheer Squad group photo shows 29 rictus-smiling, doll-like young ladies, the great majority of whom are Caucasian. This lot cheers for Men's Soccer and Women's Basketball. Finally, there's the Pom Squad, which consists of 10 Caucasian gals wearing tracksuits. They cheer and dance for Football and Men's Basketball. If you're female, white and have had high-quality orthodontic work, this clearly is the number for you. If you're not, go volunteer for the local soup kitchen, would be my advice.

The Web page also includes reams and reams of rules. I loved the language and the occasional solecism: "It cannot be stressed enough the Cheerleaders and Pom Squad members' roles as University representatives. They are highly visible symbols of Indiana University, and thus, must conduct themselves at all times as ladies and gentlemen." Apparently, being selected to the ranks of any one of these squads is considered "a prestigious honor," and the *quid pro quo* is that you cannot turn up on the job reeking of liquor or with stubble on your face. Your personal hygiene must be good; you should be well groomed. And forget body piercing!

If young people want to dress up in mini-skirts and dementedly wave over-grown feather dusters in the air, that's their business (note: radical cheerleading is becoming a fashionable form of political theater, both here and abroad). But is it IU's business? Remember, this, like most American universities, is an institution resolutely opposed to every manifestation of sexism, overt or covert, isolated or structural, imagined or real. Gender stereotyping has no place in the groves of academe; any activity that objectifies female sexuality (and cheerleading assuredly does) is to be proscribed. As a result, we have countless initiatives in place to address every possible manifestation of gender bias or inequity. Except, it would seem, when it comes to the Miss IU Pageant (reinstated after 37 years) and Bloomington's Barbie dolls. If you think I'm a whining Limey, then read what Tom Wolfe has to say in *I am Charlotte Simmons*: "They kick their legs up like cancan dancers, they show you the inside of their thighs, their breasts are hoisted up like—like—like missiles waiting for someone to push the button, they're wiggling their hips, they wear these skimpy outfits…" Don't be fooled by the seeming innocence of it all; just spend a few minutes on the Web looking at the many porn sites devoted to cheerleaders. Cheerleading is not about sport; it's about sex.

Personally, I couldn't give a fig about cheerleading: do it, don't do it, as you wish. I do, however, care that IU, along with countless other institutions of higher, and not so high, learning, is, at the very least, sending inconsistent signals, and that, at the very worst, is guilty of rank hypocrisy. Wolfe and I are not maverick male party poopers: the female co-authors of *Cheerleader! An American Icon*, don't mince their words either: "It's about sex and popularity. Every girl understands the power of the short skirt." Including, one has to say, a former Chancellor of the Bloomington campus—a lady *d'un certain âge*—who, astonishingly, participated in the annual homecoming parade though the streets of the town clad in a red, mini-skirted cheerleader's outfit. Methinks it is time to stop skirting the issue.

# BALLOONING IN BLOOMINGTON

My license plate says Crossroads of America. I think it means that lots of interstate highways slice through Indiana. For many years, I had no idea where Indiana lay on the map. It was simply one of the I-states: Iowa (with the river), Idaho (of potato fame), Illinois (think Chicago and Abe Lincoln) and Indiana (home of the Indy 500 and birthplace of the pouting James Dean). Indiana is a place bi-costal types and tourists fly over—as fast as the headwinds will allow. It's not exactly a destination point.

I recall a piece in *The Spectator* magazine not so long ago about places that sucked (that was the actual wording, and in a venerable English weekly, to boot); to my horror, the rankings began with the mid-West before moving on the Third World cities of unimaginable awfulness. It's fine for me to suggest that one would have to be crazier than a shithouse rat to live here—if I may demonstrate my command of demotic speech—but to have my weekly lifeline to Albion broadcast the fact to all and sundry certainly didn't brighten one's day.

I identify with those good Canadians interviewed by Michael Moore in *Bowling for Columbine*, who cheerfully declared that they didn't lock their doors at night. Bloomington is like Canada in that regard. Leave your front door unlocked, and the family silver is still there the next morning; leave your car unlocked and the CDs may have been pilfered—but only if it's Little Five Hundred (LFH) weekend. The LFH is the bike race which starred in *Breaking Away.* The movie was shot right outside my office, though the axle grease has long since given way to the Arboretum. The nearest Bloomington gets to a crime wave is the annual LFH gathering, when drunken students behave like drunken students. Lock up your disks if not your daughters, is my advice.

Bloomington is often referred to as an oasis. Actually, it's the Manaus of the mid-West. We have an opera season, and you'll see marvelous productions of Mozart, Donizetti and Verdi for drop-dead prices. The Metropolitan Opera Company performed in Bloomington for many years in the forties and fifties; the legendary Rudolf Bing and his team of 300 singers and support staff coming to town by train. To the best of my knowledge, no other university stage has hosted New York's finest. There's theater, jazz, cinema and all the other good things associated with a college town, not forgetting basketball. Only more, and more often than almost anywhere else on the planet. This is the town where stellar cellist Janos Starker and charismatic coach Bob Knight co-existed for donkeys' years; outspoken gods in their respective pantheons.

Bloomington has its charms, but the lady doth protest too much. Students wear near identical sweatshirts, the word "Indiana" emblazoned across their chests. At any moment they have only to lower their gaze and be reassured that there are where they yearn to be. Cotton compasses always pointing in the same direction.

We're forever telling ourselves and anyone else who will listen how fortunate we are to be here, to have music on tap and a weekly farmers' market. It's as if we're afraid we've lost our marbles by relocating to this most implausible of locations, equidistant from Little Nashville (a kitsch-loving, C&W fan's paradise) and mean, buzz-cut Martinsville (still trying to shrug off a spurious reputation for being the headquarters of the modern Ku Klux Klan).

Our city is sensibly managed, as far as I can tell. Many good citizens devote hours of their time to doing what they believe is in the best interests of the community. The city's quietly exercised charm and abundant cultural resources have made it something of a draw for retirees. Then there's Lake Monroe, man-made, to be sure, but the water's real. Lakeside camping and golf attract droves of locals and long week-enders from Illinois. On Lake Lemon, you can swim in the company of yachts, kayaks, canoes, jet skis and speedboats of every denomination. At the end of the day, though, it's still the mid-West: no mountains, no oceans and no architecture of note. But perhaps I was missing something.

Last month we took a balloon ride over Bloomington to double check. Bleary-eyed we met up with our pilot at 5 a.m. on a summer Sunday. The city was out for the count. Weather reports digested, the convoy (three vans, three balloons) trundled off into the countryside. Mist hung over the fields. A flaming sun had started its ascent. The scene was set, and perfectly. In case you don't know, ballooning is a high involvement, high maintenance activity. The passengers are roped in from the get-go. It takes a lot of huffing and puffing to get one of these things off the ground. But we did, and for ten minutes it was ethereally beautiful, our squadron of multi-colored balloons rising and dipping in a semblance of unison, three giant, helium-puffed, upside-down tear drops. One looks out over the basket, but there's no sense of fear. I couldn't stand atop a building half this height without succumbing to vertigo. We drifted as the winds decreed, surges of adroitly applied flame lifting us over hedgerows and telephone wires. But that was it. For the rest of the hour we floated aimlessly above trees. Nothing but trees, a canopy of green blanketing south central Indiana, until, finally and fortunately, we landed with the mildest of bumps in an expansive field next to a derelict farmhouse.

The pilot and I then proceeded to drag the balloon, basket and remaining on-board occupant through the savannah-like grass to the waiting chase vehicle. The grass was saturated and unyielding. The memory of the first ten minutes of matinal bliss quickly faded; sweat, grunting and dampness were all that remained. Putting a balloon back in its bag is harder than inflating the bloody thing. It takes ages, and much muscle. To celebrate our hour-long flight, the balloonist whipped out four mini-bottles of Asti Spumante which were served in Styrofoam cups—the down-home, Hoosier way—along with a potted history of ballooning, from the magnificent Montgolfier brothers to high-flying Virgin boss, Sir Richard Branson. The unexpected arrival of a near neighbor who looked and behaved disturbingly like one of the toothless rednecks in the movie *Deliverance* temporarily damped our merriment. But after a dollop of hail-fellow-well-met from our pilot, we were safely on our way back to Bloomington listening to yet more hot air about ballooning ups and downs while privately wondering if there were more trees in Indiana than the Amazon jungle.

Indiana may be the self-proclaimed Crossroads of America, but our morning's balloon ride made it abundantly clear that there is one helluva difference between an intersection and a destination point.

# ME, MINE, GIMME

THERE FOLLOWS A TRUE, IF MONUMENTALLY trivial story. Two of my colleagues took a faculty candidate to dinner. As the meal ended, one of them asked nonchalantly if her leftovers could be boxed to go—along with those of the guest. What the poor fellow from AT&T Labs made of this extraordinary combination of tastelessness and tightfistedness I shudder to think. A doggie bag—you know, the left over bones and gristle that we take home to Fido, discretely wrapped by a canine-loving waiter—is one thing; but hoovering up your companions' scraps for personal consumption...?

My musings on such matters were reactivated by the antics of our fellow diners at *Grazie*, Bloomington's routinely mispronounced but sassiest trattoria. A woman at the next table asked the waiter to not only box her unfinished salad, but to add some cheese; next the remnants of her entrée, followed by the uneaten half of her companion's supper. All were canted into purpose-built containers in front of our unblinking eyes. Three silver-foil boxes of tepid pasta and whatnot, ready to be carried smugly off into the autumn night. Now, these two tight wads hadn't supped so much as a single glass of beer or house wine between them, yet here they were demanding that the restaurant not only gift-wrap their leftovers but also add extra cheese for good measure. Talk about chutzpah!

As it happens, we had just returned from two weeks in the Veneto region of Italy and couldn't recall a single instance of food being boxed to go in the American way. It got me thinking. Why do Hoosier restaurants pile our plates with more than we can hope to eat? Why not serve a civilized portion in the first place, and put an end to the vulgarity of boxing-to-go? If diners want two dinners—a now and a then—let them pay for two dinners. There is something abject about this practice. Here's one gift horse that is always loaded greedily into the mouth. Worse: diners now believe it is their divine right to leave with a parcel of foppishly boxed seconds.

The next example of contemporary boorishness took place in Borders. It takes place there every day, but, interestingly, not in any of the big city Borders I've patronized. Espresso in hand I head to the café section to sip in peace, only to find that all the tables are occupied by students, most of whom have bought neither coffee nor comestibles from the café; certainly not any reading materials from the books section. Rather, they are working on their term papers, pecking laptops, cell phoning, or chatting breezily with near neighbors. I stared at one young offender, a bobbing-head dog with wires. She had her personal papers spread all over a table, having claim-staked three seats: one with her butt, two with her bare feet. I enquired of the Borders staff whether they had any kind of policy to ensure that *bona fide* customers might not be denied seats by those using the premises as an extension of their dorms or library carrel. Of course not. "We don't kick anyone out," came the bemused response from Kate, resting thespian and store doyenne. And so I stood, clasping my coffee, while the non-customers sat, oblivious.

How have things reached the point that some people feel it is their right to use a commercial store as a personal workspace without spending so much as a dime? We have places for that kind of thing, and they're called libraries. And Bloomington is not exactly short of libraries.

Is Borders really so desperate to maximize local in-store traffic that it'll risk the goodwill of dollar-dropping customers? Which brings me to the Borders Saturday morning crowd, the Brahmins of Bloomington spongers. I've watched this Kerry-voting coterie arrive, waffles, bagels and muffins in hand (acquired elsewhere or home-baked), grab a pile of pristine newspapers, and begrudgingly purchase a mug of the dirt-cheap coffee of the day. For an outlay of next to nothing they'll bivouac for an hour or two in the café, consume refill after refill and leave scrunched up papers for suckers like me to purchase at full cost.

Now, whether I sit or stand and grump in a bookstore café matters naught in the tide of human affairs. What does matter, though, is the metastasizing attitude that says, it's my right to have cheese added to my soon-to-be-boxed salad, my right to sit where I want when I want in your store, my right to drink endless, free refills while leafing though unpaid-for magazines. It's the kind of behavior once associated with ill-bred children, not privileged students and their professors. Apparently, free riding is what the Free World is about; at least in this neck of the Hoosier woods.

# PARKING WOES

THERE HAS NOT BEEN A PARKING-RELATED homicide on campus—
yet. I certainly wouldn't bet against a tenure-seeking professor going
postal in a university parking lot some day soon. The pressures
associated with gaining tenure coupled with the daily frustrations
of workplace parking are a Molotov cocktail waiting to be ignited.
Over the years, a body of lore has built up around the frustrations of
university parking. A former president of Dartmouth once said his
sleepless nights were the result of "fear that everyone with a parking
permit will show up at the same time." For what it's worth, we've
been reliably informed by the authorities at Indiana University that
there are enough parking spaces to go around; the only problem is
that the available parking spaces are not where we would like them
when we actually need them. As so often in life, the theory is fine;
it's just that the execution leaves something to be desired.

The modern American university has been defined as
"warring departmental fiefdoms held together by a common concern
about parking." Variations on this adage abound, though the initial
formulation should, as far as I can tell, be credited to the University of

California's Clark Kerr in his 1963 Godkin lectures at Harvard, where he described the modern university as "a collection of individual faculty entrepreneurs united by a common grievance over parking." It's as good a definition as you're likely to get. This, after all, is the man who parsimoniously defined the role of the university chancellor as providing "parking for faculty, sex for students, and athletics for alumni."

The situation in Bloomington is probably typical of campuses across the nation: thousands of students seemingly incapable of walking or cycling to and from their dorms or apartments. The sight of sorority girls driving less than half a mile in an over-muscled SUV, cell phone cupped to ear, to hog a *reserved* parking slot (the most mortal of sins) is enough to make one's blood boil. That these privileged scions of America's upper middle classes can nonchalantly absorb $30 fines must make it doubling galling to those for whom a car is a necessity of life, and for whom the $200-$300 a year parking fee is a painful outlay. It's no big deal for the parents of the *jeunesse dorée* from Chicago's North Shore (disproportionate violators, I'm reliably informed) to cover Britney's monthly fines without batting an over-painted eyelid.

The parking lots at IU house more Hummers than Arnold Schwarzenagger's garage. It's nothing less than obscene. Unearned privileges carried much too lightly much too early in life. Residential students simply don't need cars and should not be allowed to drive on campus—to hell with the hoary old environmental rationale. Spend a day in Amsterdam or Padua, Oxford or Cambridge, and what do you see? Men and women, young and old, atop bicycles. Cycling is a natural act in these (and many other) places. Here, however, it has been reclassified as a sporting activity (the empty bike lanes notwithstanding) and walking is viewed as a form of deviant behavior;

routine trips to the drycleaners or the library naturally call for four wheels and several hundred horsepower at the very least. No wonder this nation is super-sized. I didn't own a car until I was 36, and I don't seem to have suffered as a consequence. Moreover, I lived in London for ten years where parking really was an off-the-scale headache. These days I certainly don't suffer any guilt pangs as I sweep Stanley Fish-like into the main lot in my racing green XJ8. I've served my ambulatory time. And, in any case, I'm paying through the nose to park at my place of work. So, Britney, steer clear!

Parking operations have become quasi-autonomous enterprises on the nation's campuses. These days, parking is big business. We're talking millions of dollars in fines. The money flows in year round, a most welcome (and increasingly necessary) revenue stream for the administration. If you don't pay your fine, it'll be added to your student bill for the semester (if you still don't pay, you may find that you can't graduate); if you're a member of the faculty and take exception to being ticketed, the fine will simply be garnished from your next paycheck. You'll huff and puff in vain. Equal opportunity indignity is the parking *Polizei's* philosophy.

Hiking the fines achieves two outcomes: the impecunious suffer even more, while the affluent carry on as before. As an exercise in social engineering, it's dumber than dumb. The same number of cars will be scrambling for the same finite number of places. The only difference is that parking services will be more profitable. Building lots more lots is not the answer, nor is tinkering with the fines system. American families are buying cars faster than campus officials can lay asphalt. It is time to bite the proverbial bullet—not the traffic warden. That means either banning certain categories of vehicle from the campus, or prohibiting certain classes of student from driving their cars, trucks, half-tracks or whatever on campus. Or both. Such a seemingly sensible approach could, however, backfire. Students might just vote with their feet (Jeep Cherokees, more likely) and take off for another institution with more permissive parking policies. Good riddance, I say!

Money is the root of all evil, and it's no different with parking. University administrators have entered into a Faustian bargain with their "customers," and it's too late to shred the contract. But what happens when someone finally pulls a gun in one of those overcrowded lots? Or when Bloomington's equivalent of Hamptons' socialite Lizzie Grubman mows down a group of unfortunate bystanders with a customized Mercedes-Benz SUV?

# HANDY ANDY

ANDY CLARK IS A PHILOSOPHER WHO directs the Indiana University Cognitive Science Program; or did, until he decamped to take up the ancient Chair of Logic and Moral Philosophy at the University of Edinburgh. He's British, colorful (in every sense) and awfully smart. His latest opus is the wittily entitled *Natural-born Cyborgs*, a trade book from Oxford University Press (OUP). Andy thinks and writes effortlessly; at least, that's how it seems. N-b C (and here I revert to his words) is about cognitive prostheses and how plastic brains can learn to treat well-designed new tools as if they were part of the person. Who better to have at the baptism of one's new abode than this cyber guru, and author of other well-regarded tomes such as *Being There?*

We plopped into the virgin sofas—the only visible evidence of intended habitation—popped a mid-range champagne cork, filled four flutes and let our tongues wag. But the resultant buzz had less to do with the loquacity of a quartet of deracinated Europeans than the hunger of the local mosquito population. Within seconds the first Stuka-like attack had been launched. A direct hit on one of the ladies was recorded, the resultant shock propelling a brimming glass of bubbly over a pristine sofa. Moments later something similar occurred on the matching piece when Andy gently revealed the size of OUP's advance for his last book (more than a few Bloomingdale's sofas, if you must know). Our champagne stock prematurely depleted, we decided to uncork a sparkling, raspberry-flavored Belgian beer. But you can't open a beer bottle, even a Belgian one, with a sofa: remember, this is a utensil-challenged home. No corkscrews. Here we were; four academics with enough post-nominal letters to form a credible alphabet confronted with an unopened vessel that looked like a cross between a corn-fed beer bottle and a stunted jeroboam... and no way to get at the contents.

All was not yet lost. A beginner's toolbox sat in the kitchen, along with a newly acquired electrical appliance. Surely, thought I, a motorized drill could do the job of a corkscrew, and then some. Surely, too, this would be an opportunity to demonstrate one of the central theses of Andy's book, namely, that technology is a natural extension of the human body. If a monkey can quickly learn to treat a rake as an extension of its finger, think what kind of relationship Metacarpal Man could have with an electric drill. *Vorsprung durch Technik* and all that. Thus armed with my whirring prosthesis, I proceeded to drill down into the recalcitrant Belgian cork, bulbous beads of sweat forming on my nape. Out came the drill piece minus the cork. I changed to a wider bore. But no purchase. Enter Andy. Further drilling, plus the application of twice as much British *puissance*, followed by the clamping of the now-separated drill piece with a sturdy pair of pliers. Still no luck, though about half the cork had been gouged out of the bottle in this battle of attrition. "Must be something to do with the flange," mused The Philosopher King.

Further abortive attempts seemed to suggest that drill pieces were, in fact, a different species to corkscrews. Not all spirals are spirals.

Enter Josefa (Pepa) Toribio-Mateas, another fine philosopher and a cataloguer's nightmare. How many philosophers, you're now wondering, does it take to open an idiosyncratic beer bottle? The answer, in fact, is three, providing you count me as one (my primary credential being that I read the subject desultorily for four years as an undergraduate). But I am very much a pragmatist in matters philosophical. Pepa's molars having failed to make the cork budge, out of the toolbox came a hammer and a screwdriver. The screwdriver was placed on top of the cowering cork and the hammer clinically brought down on the screwdriver's head. Edward de Bono would have been proud. A slow hiss, followed by some friendly frothing and Belgium's finest was heading for our throats. I had conquered the cork. Verily, I was a natural-born cyborg, albeit one perspiring like a natural-born pig.

# THE CUT OF ONE'S JIB

TIMES AND FASHIONS CHANGE. AS A freshman at Trinity College Dublin, I was required to wear a gown on certain occasions. My knee-length black robe flowed in the breeze as I scuttled across Front Square to the Public Theatre or Dining Hall. Today, robed undergraduates are an anachronism, though the term "gown" retains its metonymic potency—at least I hope so.

Colorful robes and exotic headdress (from fez and bonnet to pill box and mortar board) still feature prominently in academic life, accompanied (though not always, it must be said) by the appropriate *sub-fusc* clothing. At the risk of stating the obvious, Bermuda shorts and polo shirts should not be worn with academic robes, nor should balloons be affixed to mortar boards. For events such as Founders Day or the university's semiannual commencement ceremonies I have two to-die-for sets of full robes (scarlet and royal blue) with bell-shaped sleeves, hoods, and soft, tasseled bonnets upon which to call. This mode of attire has considerable pedigree, going back to medieval times. The ancient universities of Coimbra and Oxford were among the first to prescribe certain kinds of academic regalia, and to this day the traditions of academic apparel are, in the main, adhered to rigorously.

In his introduction to *Academic Dress of the University of Oxford*, Sir Richard Southwood notes that academic attire "is an outward sign of the universality of universities; of their responsibility for certain timeless values essential to the freedom of enquiry: tolerance of alternative views and courage in maintaining one's own, tirelessness in the pursuit of truth and the free exchange of knowledge." Sadly, some of one's peers seem to have lost sight of these values, as they mindlessly craft unconstitutional speech codes, neuter robust debate and impose quotas of one kind or another across the nation's campuses. Perhaps these "fashionistas" of the postmodern university should wear their gowns a little more often.

In this country, there are explicit guidelines pertaining to the wearing of academic garb. The American Council on Education (ACE) has produced a document that specifies what should be worn, when, how and by whom. Over the years, the ACE's Committee on Academic Costumes and Ceremonies has periodically reviewed the costume code and made a number of modest changes. On the key issue, though, the committee is adamant: "The governing force is tradition and the continuity of academic symbols from the Middle Ages. The tradition should be departed from as little as possible…" The recommendation relating to *sub-fusc* dress is no less explicit: "Shoes and other articles of visible apparel worn by graduates should be of dark colors that harmonize with the academic costume. Nothing else should be worn on the academic gown." It was the last sentence that particularly caught my attention. This means that one cannot, for example, attach a sprig of shamrock to one's gown in order to flag one's Irishness, nor affix a lapel pin to show one's support for the Republican Party (be it GOP or IRA). Make a single exception to this rule, and we are off down the slippery slope of unbridled self-expression. Academic attire combines history, symbolism and gravitas: it is not a matter of personal style or preference. At least it wasn't until recently.

A few years ago, our then-chancellor appeared in the robing room with a Kente sash (typically made from West-African hand-woven material) draped over her academic robes. (For the record, she's Caucasian and a graduate of Harvard.) This was not altogether novel: in recent years, some African American students have taken to adorning themselves with similar accoutrements at their graduation ceremonies. But it is something else for a senior administrator to break with tradition in this way, and it is disturbing on a number of counts. First, it shows an ignorance of, if not disdain toward, the conventions of academic dress and ritual. Second, it reveals the pusillanimity of university administrators and trustees when it comes to enforcing codified standards. Third, it sets a regrettable precedent: if one group decides to differentiate itself via ethnic or ideological signifiers, what is to stop others from following suit? One can imagine a situation where graduation ceremonies across the nation become little more than multicultural jamborees to make sartorially inspired political statements. The action of our chancellor was risible and showed scant regard for the venerable traditions of a system that predates her by eight centuries and will outlive her by many more. Empty gestures of this kind have no place at solemn academic ceremonies.

I may be a fogy and in a minority on this issue, but I'm pleased to say that I am not a lone voice in the wilderness of political incorrectness. Not so long ago a federal judge ruled that school officials in Denver had the right to ban all adornments from graduation attire, which put the kibosh on the plans of black seniors to wear a multicolored Kente cloth over their graduation gowns. Bonnets and mortars boards off to the right-thinking principal of Arvada High School for sticking to his sartorial guns! And there is some historical precedent: "A decree from the university of Paris in 1339 suggests that masters and doctors were turning up to faculty meetings in flamboyant mantels and 'sleeveless tunics.' The decree threatened these casually dressed luminaries with the loss of their vote at meetings and with suspension from teaching for a whole year if they refused to leave the meeting when asked to do so." If the dastardly French could do it in the fourteenth century, it is surely now time for IU to stop the local rot.

# THE HOLY LAND

Reared in Ireland, I quickly grew accustomed to the fact that every second building was a pub. Going on a pub-crawl was strenuous, not because of the distances covered but because of the number of licensed establishments to be visited. It was your liver, not your legs that suffered. Something similar obtains in Bloomington, except here the pubs are churches: the consolation is that both your soul and your liver will be saved. For the record, the city has one Irish pub and a sprinkling of bars. But what strikes the first-time visitor are not the licensed premises, rather the astonishing number of churches dotting the landscape. When, as part of the recruiting effort, I was taken on the obligatory town tour, I commented on the fact. The locals, both Townies and Gownies, I reckoned, must be seriously God-fearing folk. If churches are an indicator of holiness, a dangerous assumption I concede, then this surely is the Mecca of Middle America.

To add some scientific rigor to my first impressions, I turned to the local telephone directory. Not only is there a lengthy alphabetic listing of all churches in Bloomington and its hinterland, but there's also a separate section arranged by denomination. It's like a buffet lunch with every conceivable form of spiritual food on the table: Baptist (Independent, Southern, etc.), Catholic, Christian Scientist, Episcopal, Free Methodist, Lutheran, Jehovah's Witness, Mennonite, Mormon, Quaker, Pentecostal-Apostolic, Presbyterian (Reformed and not), Seventh Day Adventist, Unitarian Universalist. The list goes on and on and that's without counting the various temples, mosques and synagogues that Bloomington boasts. So many ways to engage institutionally with The Other. So much variation, so many nuances, all on a seemingly simple theme. If you can't find your god among this lot, what hope have you of ever finding him (her)?

It's not just the churches that one notices. With more varieties than Heinz to choose from, the competition for congregations is fierce. No pastor wants to be faced with rows of empty pews on a Sunday morning. At the weekend the *Herald-Times* is stuffed with announcements describing the religious fare on offer. It's the American way. Madison Avenue meets its Maker. Serious and solemn though the business of religion is, the locals are not without a sense of humor. Roadside hoardings and billboards play their part in harvesting souls: "Weather report: the son is always shining." I couldn't but smile as I sped past this word play on the road to nearby Spencer. A few miles later an existential poser: "If you died today, where would you be tomorrow?" Or, how about this daub of Hoosier wit: "What's missing from CH--CH? U R." And the seasonal "Who put the Christ in Christmas?" But my favorite to date is this: "The best vitamin for a Christian is B1."

Depending on which national poll you consult, more than 90% of Americans believe in God, 85% in miracles and 75% in angels, which may explain the sign outside our local church: "WalMart is not the only saving place." Just over a third of Americans attend a church or place of worship at least once a week, but were Bloomingtonians to be surveyed, I am a confident that the attendance figure would be double the national average. Sunday morning in Bloomington is all about neatly attired couples and scrubbed families tootling in their Saturday-washed cars to and from their high-involvement, highly comforting morning services. I've heard some of my latitudinarian colleagues discuss church attendance as if places of worship were primarily sites for social interaction, not that different from the country club. And I've detected a degree of snobbery: there are some churches one simply wouldn't be seen dead in, and others where one goes to be seen, or listen to the organist. Nothing new in that, of course.

My childhood catechism told me that God was omnipresent; there was no escaping his all-seeing eye. I naïvely thought that by absconding from Catholic Ireland and lurking in the nondescript middle bits of the United States I'd be leaving all that behind, but I'd woefully underestimated the resilience of this nation's Puritanical roots. The divine is part of daily discourse in Bloomington; grown men talk about God without so much as a blush. The G-word is right up there with big abstractions like Truth, Goodness, Democracy, Justice. "God bless America" and "God is on our side" stickers proudly adorn the rear ends of macho pick-ups and buffed sedans alike. God is a force multiplier, co-opted in the imperial cause. It's all so terribly different from the incense-laden eschatology that smothers true believers in Italy, Spain and Ireland. Here, God is an instrumentality, a unifying and, it has to be said, not very complicated construct.

To my surprise, God can also be found on campus. By that I don't mean the various chaplains and religious groups with an interest in matters divine, theistic or spiritual. Before every commencement ceremony, a prayer is intoned. Students, parents and faculty rise as one, caps are doffed and heads inclined as a local vicar, priest or rabbi hijacks the proceedings for a minute. Yet, this is a public university in a nation where separation of church and state is supposedly sacrosanct. A decade or so ago, an IU law professor, Alexander Tanford, and two students took Indiana University to court on the issue—unsuccessfully. Both the district court and the 7th Circuit Court of Appeals decreed that having prayer at IU's graduation ceremony was not unconstitutional. Apparently, it's considered a settled matter; neither a case the Supreme Court will hear nor a decision it might reverse. As a spirited 1997 piece in the *IDS* put it: "The religious trappings and prayers should be back where they belong—in religious institutions, not graduation." Words which bring to mind the admonition of the Nazarene: "Render unto Caesar the things which are Caesar's, and unto God the things that are God's."

However, as anyone who has watched the mummeries of the TV evangelists knows, the moneylenders with their bouffant hair-dos have invaded the temple of God. Centuries on and still the "pennies jingle into the money-box," but this time there's no Martin Luther to raise Cain. Religion is big business, just another Big Mac to be hawked to the bulging Bible belt.

# GAY PRIDE AND PREJUDICE

LAS VEGAS IS TO GAMBLING AS Bloomington is to…homosexuality. In December 2003, Bloomington launched its "Come Out and Play" campaign, designed to promote the city as a gay-friendly community: it was mentioned during "Weekend Update" on *Saturday Night Live*, no less. If Bloomington's PRIDE Film Festival awarded Oscarettes, *Brokeback Mountain* would have swept the boards this year.

Bloomington nestles in southern Indiana, and the state of Indiana, as any psephologist who can tell a swing from a pendulum knows, is as conservative as George W. Bush is monosyllabic. One has to hand it to the citizens of Bloomington. Going down the gay destination route when all such roads lead to perfidy in the minds of the average Hoosier is something more than a Hail Mary pass; it's a full-blown rosary. But nothing is quite what it seems in Bloomington. This is the place that put sex on the map back in the nineteen forties, thanks to the pioneering research of Alfred Kinsey, himself a technocolorful bisexual. Movie buffs will know that Liam Neeson recently took Kinsey to the big screen. Local Christian fundamentalists are still trying to take the Kinsey Institute to the cleaners.

Only last week members of the Old Paths Baptist Church of Indiana congregated outside the Law School to protest against abortion and gay marriage, waving posters with eye-catchingly sensitive slogans such as "AIDS cures fags"—shades of the Progressive Era's purity movements. This, quite naturally, brought Bloomington United and Gay, Lesbian, Bisexual and Transgender representatives out in righteous counter-protest. Such are the issues that most polarize town and gown in 21st century Bloomington.

Without legendary IU president, Herman B (no period) Wells, Kinsey could not have survived in this conservative backwater. Wells staunchly supported academic freedom, acting as a lightning rod for the ire directed at the zoologist turned sexologist. In a 1953 letter to the National Council of Catholic Women, Wells defended Kinsey doughtily: "The University believes the human race has been able to make progress because individuals have the freedom to investigate all aspects of life." Knowledge, he said, "rather than ignorance, will assist mankind in the slow and painful development toward a more perfect society." Would that there were more Wellses in this world.

Here's an extract from an article in the *Indianapolis Star*: "Amazingly, someone has finally said it in print: Herman Wells, the beloved former president of Indiana University, whose lifetime of extraordinary achievements are chronicled with engaging modesty in his autobiography, *Being Lucky*, might have been gay." What took so long, I thought, when I saw this piece? I've been here all these years and have often wondered why on earth I've never heard the question posed before. Some things are plausible; others are blindingly obvious. Wells's sexual orientation (active or passive) belonged to the latter category.

I, of course, have no first hand evidence to prove my assertion, but only a deaf and blind cultural anthropologist would have failed to pick up the secondary clues. The *Star* piece also noted that Wells "never married, never dated, and as far as anyone knows, never had an intimate relationship with another man or woman." All of which led to considerable speculation over the years: "Was Herman Wells a homosexual?" The newspaper described the mere asking of this question as "explosive." It didn't say why (*autres temps, autres moeurs*?), but I suspect that the real reason is that in Bloomington, Wells's name and memory are sacrosanct. Hear no evil, see no evil, speak no evil: the Bloomington *omertà*. As with Martin Luther King Jr., hagiography has no truck with human frailty or normative deviation. King (invariably and preferentially granted the prefix Dr.) was a womanizer and a plagiarist, and Wells (occasionally referred to, affectionately, as St. Herman) may have been gay. None of which detracts one iota from these two gentlemen's extraordinary contributions to the life of this nation. But, for some, it inconveniently muddies the memory. Biography must never get in the way of hagiography.

Wells lived with his mother and employed houseboys; you'd have to be daft not to figure that he might just have had latent homosexual tendencies. After all, if Kinsey's data are anything to go by, then a lotta folk ain't straight—including the benchmarking Kinsey himself. Even if Wells had been as queer as a coot, as we used to say in 1960s Ireland, it wouldn't have added to or detracted from his accomplishments as the second longest-serving president of IU. He made Indiana University the place that it is. Who knows, perhaps the explanation for his (and IU's) success is somehow linked to his presumptive gayness. But for such an obvious question—Was he? Wasn't he?—not to have been asked in a small-minded, mid-

Western town is simply inconceivable. Has there been a conspiracy of silence?

Long before Bloomington decided to position itself as a gay destination, and long before the launch of BloomingOUT, Indiana's first and only locally produced gay, lesbian, bisexual and transgender-themed radio program, one could sense an uncommon acceptance of alternative lifestyles, the spluttering rage of local politicians notwithstanding. It came home to me in a variety of ways: casual same-sex displays of public affection on and off campus; the knowing asides and glances at university receptions and *soirées*; being introduced without so much as a flicker of irony or self-consciousness to a bearded chap wearing a string tie by a male professor as follows: "Have you met my wife?"—and this years before gay marriage had registered on the national political agenda. A sub-culture existed within the university and announced itself ever so subtly. Remember the clerihew written about the brilliant gay logician Alan Turing: "Turing / Must have been alluring / To get made a don / So early on"?

On the surface, most of one's male peers (like most but not all giraffes, some of which are openly gay) seemed to be anchored in conventional heterosexual relationships, married with children, though one did wonder whether some of these were *marriages de convenance*. A playful glimpse behind local lace curtains was provided by Joan Peyser in her biography of Leonard Bernstein. The maestro was a noted homosexual in his later years and during a six-week spell in Bloomington in 1982 wrote a parody to be sung to the tune of "A bicycle built for two." This Bernstein dedicated and sang to none other than the then dean of the IU music school at one of the several student parties they attended. The ditty went as follows:

Deany, weeny, show me your penie, do!

I'm all steamy, all for the love of you!

You want to see mine? It's teeny!

But that's 'cause I'm a sheeny—

But you're a goy,

And boy oh boy!

I'll just betcha it's built for two!

Had Wells attracted and recruited faculty to some extent in his own image, consciously or otherwise? Did his early *protégés*, in turn, hire in their image? In retrospect, it certainly seems as if President Wells anticipated the 21st century *Zeitgeist* by half a century, but had he done so by chance or by design? Don't ask me. Ask the dwindling number of Wells men. For it is they who are uniquely qualified to say how an oasis of sexual tolerance formed in the conservative heartland long before "destination management" had entered the marketeer's odious lexicon.

# ET IN ARCADIA EGO

IF YOU THINK POLITICAL CORRECTNESS IS old hat, you should see some of the dreck that lands on my desk. A 10-page report that attempts to "measure the state of diversity" at Indiana University. Via email, an invitation to a talk given by a professor of education entitled, "Creating a culturally responsive learning environment for students of color." On the front page of the *IDS* the headline reads: "Student complaints lead to Christmas tree ban in building atrium." And this a year before Fox News decides it is high time to put the Christ back in Xmas. The *Chronicle of Higher Education* carries a story: "Feminist author says famous professor sexually harassed her at Yale in 1983." (At least it wasn't 1883.) On a listserv I am exhorted to place a Safe Zone sticker on my office door: "This zone is declared safe! Regardless of race, ethnicity, national origin, gender, sexual orientation, religion, age, and ability, you will be treated and respected as a human being." Just arrived, the Affirmative Action plan for the campus which is a whopping 140 pages of tables and minority hiring targets—a numerologist's delight. Via internal mail a snot-green poster asking: "Are you concerned about sexual harassment?" And so it goes on, day in day out; fusillades of bilge launched by armies of agelastic apparatchiks. *"Ecrasez l'infâme!"* —to use Voltaire's words.

Banning Christmas trees because some neurasthenic students feel "excluded" is reverse discrimination of the silliest kind, while plastering Safe Zone stickers on doors is best left to tiresome teens. But this is a world in which Gingerbread Man cookies have been gender neutralized: the Indiana Memorial Union now sells only Gingerbread Person cookies. How can matters have reached such a sorry state? How can otherwise intelligent human beings think that something as diffuse and multi-dimensional as diversity can be measured as if one were taking the temperature of water? Is there no statute of limitation on Naomi Wolf's claims of sexual harassment against the octogenarian Harold Bloom? Where will the insanity end?

In the course of the last decade, campus diversity initiatives and offices have erupted like acne across the face of higher education, consuming untold millions of dollars that should properly be directed at teaching and research. It's a veritable industry with its own costive lexicon and po-faced enforcers. Here in Bloomington we have an Office of Diversity Education, but that is depressingly unexceptional, even if the Orwellian nomenclature varies from institution to institution. There are platoons of "diversiphiles" determined to control the culture and climate (two of their pet words) of the modern university, ironically creating an environment that is as deficient in genuine diversity as it is in humor. Occasionally, though, a shaft of common sense pokes through the fustian. Let me illustrate with two pieces from the *IDS*. The first described an anti-affirmative action cookie sale on campus where white males were charged $1 per cookie, females 75 cents, Hispanics 50 cents and African Americans

25 cents. You get the point? One can well imagine the reaction that this instructional jape provoked. The second was an unusually clear-headed editorial in the *IDS* triggered by the soporific sound bites of diversity ideologues. The title of the staff editorial said all that needed to be said: "Deflating diversity: University emphasis on diversity drains life from the word."

I sometimes wonder what the Townies make of all this guff, assuming they, in fact, notice anything at all beyond the pennants proclaiming "1 for Diversity" that flutter futilely on the fringes of the campus. Few—certainly not the Board of Trustees—delve deep enough into the university's Web site to discover the Diversity Educator's homepage, where the visitor is greeted by a less than pacific quotation from Malcolm X's "The Ballot or the Bullet Speech." Which is probably just as well. The university, despite some well-meaning efforts to make itself more hospitable to minorities of all kinds, is still predominantly Caucasian (only 4% African American, 3% Asian and 2% Hispanic). But that shouldn't come as a shock or constitute a pretext for endless self-flagellation. After all, the city of Bloomington itself (87% white, 4% African American, 5% Asian and 2-3% Hispanics or Latino) is hardly the number one port of call for the average African American, given that this part of the mid-West was notoriously supportive of the Ku Klux Klan: Bloomington's last lynching was in the 1930s. Memories persist.

But, its whiteness notwithstanding, Indiana University, Bloomington, is commendably cosmopolitan, with students from virtually every nation on earth roaming the campus. The late President Wells somehow transformed a regional university into a truly international one during his remarkable lifetime, a tradition continued under the suave leadership of the ambassadorial Patrick O'Meara: today there are roughly 3,300 foreign students on the

Bloomington campus alone. This, by the way, has greatly increased the entertainment and fine dining options available to the local citizenry; Bloomington not only hosts the hugely popular Lotus Festival of World Music every year but also boasts a superabundance of exotic restaurants: Tibetan, Korean, Turkish, Japanese, Thai and Moroccan, in addition to many more. Rhythms and food poisoning to suit every taste. And all this so close to the Mason-Dixon line.

It's a cliché, but, nonetheless, true: Bloomington is a cultural oasis, albeit one that frets more about pigmentation and ethnic labeling than it should. We would do well to recall the words of journalist and PBS commentator, Richard Rodriguez: "The interesting thing about Hispanics, of course, is that you never meet a Hispanic in Latin America...You meet Chileans and Peruvians and Mexicans. You do not meet Hispanics...Hispanics is rather one of those strange gringo contrivances like flavorless salsa that you find only in Dallas, Texas" Well, the groves of academe are replete with strange gringo contrivances, though I'm not sure that the good citizens of Bloomington give a hoot. I just wish my colleagues weren't so uncritically accepting of the flavorless salsa that is diversity dogma. But I fear I am pissing in the wind, as this flaccid email suggests: "Last year, the School decorated some public areas for the season. This year, we won't be displaying symbols specific to any one tradition in our lobbies or lounges. We hope staff will continue to express seasonal cheer in their own work areas. In areas where we have significant student traffic, it's best to keep decorations as neutral as possible."

Let it be bruited abroad that Salsa Claus is alive and well in Bloomington and wishes you a very neutral Christmas.

# B+ FOR BLOOMINGTON

"AND THE SECOND RUNNER-UP IS…" ONCE upon a time there was a winner and a runner-up: Victor Ludorum and Also Ran. Life was simple. Language had meaning. Today, we have runners-up to the power of *n*, whether it's the Miss America pageant or the local agricultural fair. "*Everybody* has won, and all must have prizes," as the Dodo said in *Alice in Wonderland*. Losing has been airbrushed out of existence. That way, no one's feelings get hurt. I first noticed the trend many years ago at the Monroe County Fair, where Gownies were decidedly thin on the ground and *all* pies in the apple pie competition had received splendid rosettes. Even the most desiccated and malformed specimen warranted recognition. Bathing beauties or baked beauties, everyone is a winner in today's "feel-good" world. We're applauded for taking part, for expressing a view, for being inadequate and for failing. Mere participation, in our postmodern culture, merits a prize.

What holds for the county fair also holds for academia. We call it grade inflation. Our students are crestfallen if awarded anything lower than a *B+* for their course work, despite the fact that

$B+$ equates with "very good." But being "very good" is not good enough, if you've been raised on a diet of $A$'s and the attendant belief that anything less is tantamount to failure. So, rather than deal with suicidal students and muttered threats of litigation, we delude ourselves with the comforting thought that Lake Wobegone can be replicated across the nation's campuses. We're all excellent, and the bell curve be damned! But there is a knock-on effect: bright students are clamoring for the introduction of a new grade, $A++$, to distinguish real merit from feel-good merit. The corrosive effect of this trend came home to me forcibly when my daughter (then at elementary school) announced proudly that she had scored 103 on a test with a maximum (i.e., perfect) score of 100. We're launched on an inflationary spiral that insults common sense, but is designed to make us feel good about ourselves: Carmen certainly did.

But there is still some uncommonly good common sense to be found in these parts. I live, as I never tire of telling friends around the world, in what amounts to a mid-sized university town, still best known, it sometimes seems, for the oafish antics of its erstwhile basketball coach. These islands of intellect are quintessentially American and Bloomington is a confounding blend of corn and cosmopolitanism. Grand opera (courtesy of the Music School) and magnums of Château Latour (available from Big Red, *the* local liquor store) live cheek by jowl with red necks and fried catfish. Here, town and gown cannot pass like ships in the night: their fates are entangled.

In the center of this particular island is what at first glance appears to be a modestly sized wannabe airport terminal, architecturally just the right side of neo-brutalism; it is, in fact, the Monroe County Public Library. You can't miss it, which is probably just what the architect and staff were counting on. Its location on

Kirkwood Avenue, scene of Friday night cruising—low riders with neon strips and throaty mufflers; country kids with Stetsons, Wranglers and self-consciously carried attitude—is, arguably, its most important asset. Once inside, the interior design does its work. The building is spacious, luminous and accessible—just like an airport. And the people (those lurking behind desks) seem genuinely eager to assist. As far as I can tell, there isn't a single "Silence please" sign blighting the landscape. Again, just like an airport. In short, the building doesn't conform to the popular stereotype; or, to put it another way, it does: your interpretation will, naturally, reflect your particular parcel of prejudices.

Anyway, my children love it, and they're not without a modicum of discrimination. They can tell Harry Potter from Calvin and Hobbes at thirty paces. Nor are they blind to the blandishments of the local Barnes & Noble, from whom libraries could learn a few lessons in the art of engineering ambience. For the children, it's not a case of either/or. But that shouldn't come as a surprise: for years researchers have told us that book buyers and book borrowers are by and large the same population.

I've ambled around this space in tow and thrall. I actually thought of tape-recording the children's casual remarks and observations as they went about their business (it's the cultural anthropologist *manqué* in me, I guess), but then thought the better of it. They know how to navigate the space; they seem manifestly at ease and grateful for what's on offer. They find stuff and stimulation. Going to the library constitutes a treat. It's not something they do because there are no bookstores, because we can't afford to buy books, or because their school doesn't have a library/media center. A trip to the library is something in its own right; an experience to be anticipated and enjoyed. It's the combination of space—safe space and stuff—and the fact that one can take the stuff home by the ton and for free. Why wouldn't kids be attracted to libraries? And why wouldn't taxpayers see the wisdom of subsidizing the reading habit in the young? It's a "no brainer." Hats off to the Bloomington city fathers. *B*+ all round.

# SIGN LANGUAGE

For many years Thomas Sebeok was an *eminence énorme* on the Bloomington campus. The paterfamilias of North American semioticians, Sebeok remained an outrageously productive scholar right up to his eighty-first year. Born in Budapest in 1920 and educated at the universities of Cambridge, Chicago and Princeton, he was brought to Bloomington in 1943 by the wily Mr. Wells, where he remained until his death in 2001. By the time I joined IU, Tom was a veritable institution. His list of accomplishments, publications and honors was humbling: his affability and lack of pomposity all the more appealing for that. For years Tom brunched in his favorite booth at the Uptown Café—exposed brick and Gumbo—holding court and regaling his companion *du jour* with easy erudition and mischievous wit. He'd often reminisce, and the names of renowned scholars of the twentieth century whom he'd met or with whom he had traded intellectual blows would roll off the tongue. It was name dropping of sorts, I suppose, but never self-conscious or self-serving. This man walked among giants. And what a joy it was to listen, as the conversation veered from his work on animal communication and biosemiotics to childhood memories of his father routinely conducting his business affairs in a pre-war Budapest café. *Tel père, tel fils*.

One of Sebeok's best-known books is *A Sign Is Just a Sign* (hum it to the tune of *As Time Goes By* from the movie *Casablanca* was his wry recommendation), which is as useful a place as any to get to grips with the core concepts of semiotics—the science of signs. The good professor Sebeok may have resided in Bloomington for almost half a century, but I seriously doubt if anyone in the city's Parks & Recreation Department has ever read any of his writings or taken Semiotics 101. On the other hand…maybe, just maybe, someone saw the title of his book and took it literally. At least that's what I thought the first time I went for a walk along Clear Creek Trail on the edge of town: two miles of meandering black top, edged with trees, a stream and several ugly housing developments.

The so-called trail is popular with power walkers, waddlers, strollers, skaters and bumbling bikers. It's all terribly twee apart from the occasional hobble-de-hoy, but better than nothing for those with a hankering after the great outdoors. The distinguishing feature of this recreation facility is neither the local flora nor fauna; it is the signage. It starts with a brace instructing dog owners on how to handle feces and another telling us not to leave valuables in our cars. It's not just the staggering number of signs per furlong, but also the miscellany of symbols and content. The signs—all carrying the words "Clear Creek Trail" across the top for hikers and others afflicted with Alzheimer's—appear every hundred yards or so along this manufactured walk, providing a welter of information that is by turns redundant, comical or semantically challenging. To make matters worse, the signs are luridly painted (aquamarine, green, white and red) and a blight on the already somewhat blighted environment:

worse still, they are inescapable and infantilizing. When the trails bends to the left there is a sign with a curved arrow; when the trail curves right, there's a right-bending arrow framed by a red triangle. It is, I need hardly say, blindingly obvious where the trail is going, but someone in Parks & Rec. nonetheless felt a need to state the obvious, sign-wise. Underfoot things are just as bad; messages, courtesy of the Parks people (logo plus full name of the department in every case), tell us incessantly and pointlessly how far we are from some roundabout or other.

Signs tell you that you are approaching the end of the trail when the end is already in sight. Others depict a cow in a red triangle. Underneath it says "300 feet" and underneath that ("100 M") which, presumably, means meters rather than moos. Two hundred feet later the same sign but with the words "100 feet." These, as far as I can tell, refer to cattle which may once upon a time have crossed this path but have long since become beef burgers. I have yet to see a calf let alone a cow. But the signs are still there, telling you, that the cow is getting closer. James Joyce comes to mind: "Once upon a time and a very good time it was there was a moo-cow coming down along the road and this moo-cow that was coming down along the road met a nicens littleboy named baby tuckoo..."

There is another one nearby with the words STOP AHEAD in a red chevron. This is followed a hundred yards later with a further injunction. An image of a man walking towards another man atop a bike along with the word STOP (now a red square, not a chevron). Given that the trail at this point is about to intersect a busy road with vehicular traffic, stop is what most sane folk would likely do. But apparently the Parks & Rec. Department think we can't think for ourselves, so taxpayer dollars are wantonly transmuted into signs that fail to state the obvious unambiguously.

The *pièce de résistance* is the stuff of a semiotician's wet dream. By the time you've deconstructed the message, you've either been mown down by an iPod on rollerblades or collided concussively with a fellow pedestrian equally mesmerized by the runic sign. This semiotic conundrum consists of an inverted red triangle with the words YIELD TO at the center. Three arrows point to the three angles of the triangle, where three symbols are located: a pedestrian, a bicycle and a roller skate. Even the boffins from Bletchley Park would have needed a few minutes to crack this one. At first I thought it was a coded instruction to cyclists to run down errant pedestrians and selfish skaters, but, in fact, the sign, I finally concluded, is designed to establish a rights hierarchy: in-line skaters give way to pedestrians and cyclists, who, in turn, give way to skaters. The irony, of course, is that such signs are more likely to cause the kinds of collisions they seek to prevent than if there were no signs at all—a conclusion reached by the enlightened citizens of Christianfield in Denmark where road signs and stop lights were removed in an effort to make drivers themselves responsible for being attentive. It's known in the trade as "psychological traffic calming."

A sign may, indeed, be just a sign, as Tom Sebeok playfully maintained, but, unfortunately, Tom didn't live long enough to become acquainted with the semiotic silliness of Clear Creek. Had he, his book might have been titled differently.

# BASS FISHING AND BEETHOVEN

MOST MAJOR UNIVERSITIES HAVE SCHOOLS OF law, business, medicine and so on. Not many have a School of Health, Physical Education and Recreation: IU does, and it was, in fact, the first of its kind in the U.S. This polycephalous beast, phonetically known as hyper, as in "bolic", and acronymically as HPER, has its fingers in an amazing variety of pies. In addition to educating the next generation of Hoosiers about such fashionable notions as wellness and healthy living, the School of HPER operates a motley collection of centers and institutes, including the Bradford Woods Outdoor Center, Hilltop Gardens and Nature Center, National Center on Accessibility, and Rural Center for AIDS/STD Prevention. HPER, it would appear, is where town and gown converge, figuratively and literally speaking.

No one could accuse HPER of being an ivory tower. Its official bulletin is splendidly anti-elitist. I don't think I've ever encountered such a smorgasbord of credit-bearing courses on offer from a single academic unit. If you're interested in "Hazardous Materials and Waste Control," "Death and Dying," "Advanced Human Nutrition," or "Therapeutic Horticulture," this is the place for you. If you fancy a bit of real-world experience on the side there's the "Practicum in College Sex Education," or, for the more morbidly inclined, how about the "Practicum in College Death Education"?

For jocks there is an advanced, yes, *advanced*, 3-credit course on "Strapping and Bandaging of the Physically Active." Archaeologists presumably have a course of their own for mummy wrapping. But it gets even better when you turn to the Physical Activity Instruction Program course listing. This is where the average Joe's heart will skip a beat. If you want to brush up on your side-walk or shim-sham, there's "Beginning Tap Dance;" if a placid evening's fishing is your idea of heaven, then HPER has just the course for you: "Basic and Innovative Techniques for Catching Large Mouth Bass." You should know that when they're not catching or scoffing catfish, a local delicacy, Hoosiers are often to be found reeling in bass at nearby Lake Monroe. Bass fishing, I've also come to learn, is not just a leisure-time activity; it's a serious business with professional anglers, a competition circuit, TV coverage and non-trivial prize money. All of which makes me think that HPER is no slouch when it comes to developing market-relevant courses and connecting with the community.

Nor is our esteemed School of Music averse to a little populism. Over the years, both jazz and rock 'n roll have elbowed their way into the curriculum despite the protestations of some traditionalists. As Terry Eagleton remarks in *After Theory*: "In the old days, rock music was a distraction from your studies; now it may well be what you are studying." Among the most popular courses on campus, as the wait lists will testify, are "History of Rock Music I and II," described by one enthusiastic student as "really interesting, compared to something like biology." Alongside Bach, Brahms and Bartok you'll now find John, Paul, George and Ringo. There are courses on, for instance, "The Music of Jimi Hendrix", "The Beach Boys, Beefheart & the Residents." Even better, devotees of the Fab Four can opt for "Overseas Study: The Beatles in London," a summer session offering through the IU International Office. Posing for photos at the St. John's Wood zebra crossing outside the famed recording studio is *de rigueur*.

Thanks to the efforts of noted music professor, composer and rock history textbook author, Glenn Gass, IU's School of Music has boldly gone where no other conservatory has gone before...down the Yellow Brick Road. The appeal of Gass's classes can only be enhanced by his guest list, which over the years has included icons (or icons-by-association) such as Lou Reed, Neil Young, Mrs. Buddy Holly and local-boy-made-good, John Mellencamp, and by having celebrity rock drummer, Kenny Aronoff (who has performed with Meat Loaf, no less) as an adjunct professor.

One can understand the professor's excitement at having a rock star at his side, but describing Mr. Mellencamp's appearance in the classroom as "like having Beethoven come out in a music appreciation class" is perhaps taking things too far. One trusts that Gass's tongue was wedged firmly in his cheek when he went on to tell the *IDS* that Mellencamp "has got such a social conscience and moral authority." Whatever else our latter day Beethoven may have, it is neither a way with words nor moral authority. Here, for example, is what the celebrity guest had to say about his interactions with the students: "I don't know that I really relate to them on any particular level because I am very up front, very blunt, so I don't know if they are used to that in a college situation." Come again?

Well, the swaggering rock star *is* very up front and blunt. I know because I was seated behind him the day Indiana University in its wisdom awarded him an honorary doctorate: he's a generous donor. Mellencamp was inappropriately dressed in a bog-standard T-shirt and, as he rose to deliver his banal remarks to the assembled masses in Memorial Stadium, he removed a piece of chewing gum from his mouth and chucked it in the general direction of the student orchestra at the foot of the platform party. Very Beethoven! Come to think of it, even a large mouth bass would have a finer sense of decorum.

# KNIT ONE, PURL ONE

"WHAT'S YOUR ERDÖS NUMBER?" ASKED THE logician to my left. Three weeks earlier I would have looked at him blankly or stared straight ahead at my gazpacho praying that he or the question (though not the soup) would go away. Fortuitously, I knew all about Paul Erdös (*pr.* air dish) and was chomping at the bit. I'd read Paul Hoffman's delightful biography, *The Man Who Loved Only Numbers*, a few weeks earlier and I'd also had the good luck to meet a professor who not only knew but had actually accommodated the prodigiously peripatetic, engagingly eccentric Hungarian mathematician in his home. Erdös roamed the globe ceaselessly, turning up unannounced at the offices and abodes of mathematical colleagues" "My brain is open," he would declare gnomically on arrival with his life's possessions stuffed into a battered suitcase and his trademark orange plastic bag.

So, not only could I look my dinner table companion squarely in the eye, but I could also boast proudly that one of my junior colleagues—bless her Teutonic heart—had an Erdös number of two. Nods of approval all round. I'd survived the first course by virtue of knowing that an Erdös number of one is for anyone who co-authored with the Great Man; an Erdös number of two goes to anyone who has co-authored with any of those who co-authored with Erdös in the first instance, and so on. If you can't find a connection through co-authorship links, your Erdös number is infinite, in which case you probably don't want to show your face at a math convention or a Bloomington dinner party. Having a small Erdös number is a big deal.

Those inhabitants of Bloomington not busy calculating Erdös numbers are likely to be engaging in a post-prandial game of *Six Degrees of Kevin Bacon*, named after the Hollywood film star. The idea is simple: take any actor or actress (node, in math speak) and connect him or her with Kevin Bacon (another node) through movies (links) they were in with other people and hook up your chosen actor with Mr. Bacon in six steps or less (the network). Movie buffs and trivia freaks doubtless love this low-tech exemplar of participatory pop culture, even if the sociometric significance of the exercise never so much as occurs to them.

There is a serious side to all this Bacon and Erdös stuff. The science of networks has become one of the hottest topics in academia. Researchers are scrambling to understand the self-organizing properties of networks and complex systems of all kinds. It's as if the secret of life is waiting to be unlocked. Popular books pour forth on these abstruse matters, none more popular or more readable than Professor Barabási's *Linked*. If you want to know how everything is connected to everything else, and in plain English, this is *the* place to go.

It may or may not be that exciting to discover that I know someone who knows someone who knows someone who knows Umberto Eco or Paris Hilton, but it sure as hell is exciting to know that such scale-free network properties are universally observable. The webs of interconnection that Notre Dame's Barabási and others have begun to lay bare demonstrate the wisdom of the old adage, "It's not what you know, it's who you know."

That, presumably, is the thinking behind *Facebook,* a Web-based directory that connects millions of college students at Bloomington and elsewhere through social networks. This means that if you are a student you can use the service to find fellow students at either your own or another institution who share interests (mooning, body painting, philology, NASCAR racing), have courses in common or whatever. It's a simple, if crude way, of augmenting your social networks: much easier than joining the Masons or being admitted to Sigma Delta Tau. The need to be connected—witness the rise and rise of the cell phone, email and instant messaging—is seemingly insatiable. To be is to be connected. Connectedness is now an end-in-itself for millions of youngsters growing up with *Facebook, MySpace* and such like.

But it's not all hi-tech connectivity. Bloomington is experiencing a parallel, craft-based communication revival of sorts. These days the soothing murmur, "Knit one, purl one," accompanied by the click, clack of dueling needles, can be heard in neighborhood coffee shops. Knitting is back. Bloomington now has its own branch of Stitch 'n Bitch, an ecumenical group that welcomes cross-stitchers and crochet queens along with straight knitters. It meets weekly, knits, chats and maintains a Weblog of sorts. This developing sub-culture also includes the Knitting Librarians (talk about stereotype busting!).

When one thinks about it, *Facebook* is a way of knitting young people together, of creating social ties and extending community connections. In Bloomington, as elsewhere, social knitting is happening, both virtually and physically, on screen and in coffee shops. The tools and ties that bind are at once visible and invisible. Keep on clicking. Alexis de Tocqueville and his digital age *Doppelgänger*, Bernard-Henri Levy, would surely applaud.

# TWO CULTURES

A FORMER JOURNALISM DEAN ONCE CONFESSED to me that he was "overworked and overpaid." It's a line I've used many times since. As it happens, I think I am well paid, both relatively and absolutely; moreover for doing a job I rather like. Overwork is, and always has been, an occupational hazard in universities, but for my generation the life of the mind was never seen as a fast track to wealth or fame. Far from it!

Things have changed considerably, for the better and the worse. The good news is that we don't have to sew patches onto the elbows of our long-serving Harris tweed jackets or drive pre-owned Honda Civics. Our improved salaries just about keep pace with inflation such that most of us can just about keep up with last year's fashion and aspire to a gleaming new Saturn. (Administrators' pay, according to the *Chronicle of Higher Education*, has outpaced inflation for the last nine years.) Some professors, in fact, can afford to set sartorial standards: if your field is corporate strategy or constitutional law, you'll likely be wearing Hugo Boss or Cole Haan with cashmere socks; if you're a specialist in nineteenth century

Portuguese literature you won't be—not, of course, that you'd want
to be seen dead in such clobber.

The age of the "poster prof" has well and truly dawned.
"Academostars," taking a leaf out of the ancient sophists' book,
command breathtaking salaries, negotiate "golden hellos," demand
reduced teaching loads, and expect regular sabbaticals. Sign-on
fees (euphemistically referred to as set-up or discretionary funds),
housing assistance, jobs for trailing spouses and partners and
research or travel funds are all par for the recruiting course. Letters
of offer to members of the glitterati have degenerated into quasi-
legal contracts, specifying every detail of the dowry right down
to the tiniest perquisite. The idea of a "gentleman's agreement" is
lamentably and laughably anachronistic. These days, everything has
to be documented, signed and filed in triplicate. It's only a matter of
time before the superstars start employing agents to negotiate the
terms and conditions of their contracts.

Don't be fooled by the "We're cutting to the bone" rhetoric
of psittaceous administrators, as they plead for yet more public
and private support. "Bone," I've learned, is a relative construct.
Parts of academe are awash with money, while others are indigent.
C.P. Snow's "two cultures" has taken on another layer of meaning
on the modern campus. The personal research funds of some
professors are greater than the annual salaries of others. There are
slum dwellings in the groves of academe, but we pass over the fact
in silence. To understand what is meant by the term distributive
injustice you need only consult the national salary data published
annually by the *Chronicle*. It's easy to see where the bucks stop:
medicine, engineering, business and law. These are the heavy-hitting
departments, where six-figure salaries (the first digit is as likely to be
a two or three as a one) are routine. In the case of medicine, earnings

sometimes break the seven-figure barrier, dwarfing those of even the best-paid university presidents—whose remuneration packages are beginning to look a lot like those of the average CEO. In 2004, the number of college presidents earning $500,000 or more in private and public universities was 42 and 17, respectively.

These trends have not gone unnoticed at the local level. Every year the *Herald-Times* publishes the names and salaries of the university's top earners. This is front-page stuff, an absolute must-read for both the grits and gravy brigade and the muesli-munching professorate. Last year's story featured the names of all those earning $200K + (I can remember when the bar was set at a paltry $100K). The names of the Masters and Mistresses of the Universe are writ large for all to see. Some gloat, many seethe. Those who live on the wrong side of the tracks probably want to rip up the tracks and hurl them through the portals of Bryan Hall, where the administrative élite roosts. Those who provide the clerical and technical support upon which our careers necessarily rest must find it difficult to bite their tongues. The disparity between the dons and the doers is wide, and yearly widening. And it's there for all to see in the pages of the local newspaper.

But you'll also struggle to find humanities professors on this list. Come to think of it, you'll struggle to find professors of any ilk, bar a few local superstars who have shattered academe's other glass ceiling. In fact, many of the university's best-paid employees are not academics at all. In an obscene reversal of values, we pay our coaches (football, basketball, etc.) and the squads of professional administrators (think of all the suits in marketing, communications, and public relations who clog up the institutional arteries with their tumid prose) more than we pay our faculty. IU is by no means the worst offender in this regard, but that is of little consolation. I don't know whether the *Herald-Times* publishes salary data because it makes for a good story or because the editor feels impelled to let the citizens of Bloomington know what is going on in their bookish backyard. If the idea is to shame the university into smoothing out some of the more blatant inequities, the tactic has not worked. As we shall see, IU continues to pay its underperforming coaches severance packages that would keep the average Bloomington household afloat for the best part of a decade.

What does such wantonness say to local construction worker braving the climatic extremes of Bloomington or to an assistant professor of English on $50,000 a year teaching a class of 60 undergraduates? Well, it says to me that some of our over-paid colleagues would be well advised to pick up a copy of *Webster's New Collegiate Dictionary* and check the meaning of the words "bone" and "cutting" before insulting our collective intelligence with their weasel words.

# TO FAIL IS TO SUCCEED

A FEW COLLEGE FOOTBALL COACHES ARE paid $2 million per annum. Next year, twenty or thirty will be pulling down salaries of $2 million or more. I heard it on NPR: it must be true. That's an awful lot of money for teaching kids how to throw a ball. The university presidents who hire these touchline tyrants will be lucky if they earn a third of that.

Hoops and gridiron generate big revenues and big revenues command monster salaries. At IU, as elsewhere, brawn matters more than brains—if remuneration is an index of prevailing social values. Forget *Chariots of Fire*, this is the age of enticements, endorsements and executive suites. Despite being seriously in the red a few years ago, IU's Athletics Department spent a cool $220,000 refurbishing the athletic director's suite. (The director in question has, of course, since moved on.) That's as much as the average IU professor's house would fetch on the open market. Imagine what the refurbishment bill would have been had the department not been in the red. For good measure, the Athletics Department also spent more than $112,000 on a new IU logo design. Here, logos come and go almost as often as football coaches. I've forgotten the convoluted rationale the over-paid image-makers used to justify this wheeze, but one winces knowing what these marketing makeover artists pocketed for their services.

It's all so different on the other side of the Atlantic. There, balls are punted, bowled and swatted by eager young things across pitches, parks and lawns. Laps are run and lengths rowed, old rivalries renewed, "blues" awarded, and academic life goes on. There's a bit of coaching on the side, but it's all really rather easy going, quintessentially amateurish. Sport is, well, sport, a secondary activity: *Mens sana in corpore sano.*

When I interviewed at Bloomington back in 1990, a salivating realtor drove me around the city, dutifully pointing out areas where one might wish to set up home. I recall being taken through the most self-confidently vulgar estate I'd ever seen (mock Tudor and *faux* Federal jousting for attention) and being shown the very house where "Coach Knight used to live." "Who?" I asked politely. And with that I was introduced (anecdotally) to the living legend.

The protracted, long-overdue, media-hyped ouster of rambunctious basketball coach Bobby Knight took a financial toll on the university. Mr. Knight was to be paid deferred compensation of $425,000 a year for eight years. God alone knows what the university's legal fees must have been as the litigious Knight filed suit after suit. There were a lot of unhappy campers when the then president announced that Coach Knight would be parting company with the institution to which his name had become reflexively associated. That was the only time that things got out of hand in Bloomington. Rioting students expressed their displeasure in the way that rioting students traditionally do, by senselessly smashing property and themselves. Providing police protection for the president and his campus home was not an over-reaction. Things got ugly.

Bobby Knight was followed by Mike Davis, one of a small number of African American college coaches nationwide. Coach Davis must have had a good lawyer. He negotiated a six-year contract worth, potentially, $900,000 a year. In fairness, the university's base salary contribution is set at $225,000, plus $25,000 in deferred compensation. The rest is made up from sponsorship deals and media income. However—and here's the rub—any shortfall has to be covered by IU. But that's not the whole story. If my information is correct, there is the possibility of an additional incentive payment of almost $140,000 based on game results and the student athletes' grades. If the team's mean grade point average (GPA) exceeds 2.3 (on a four-point scale), yet more dollars flow to Mr. Davis. In other words, he gets paid even more for doing what he was paid to do in the first place, and, moreover, if the team's GPA rises above 3.3, a further bonus kicks in.

Surely, what's good for the sporting goose is good for the scholarly gander. What if professors had their remuneration tied to the mean GPA of their students, the number of graduating students, the frequency with which doctoral students presented conference papers, the number of NSF (National Science Foundation) and other grants they secured, their publication record, and such like? What if they solemnly promised to remain at IU until whenever in the face of all other blandishments? You get my drift? Obviously Mary Sue Coleman understands the realities of contractual life; the incumbent president of the University of Michigan has a compensation package that includes a retention bonus of $500,000 if she remains president for the full five years of her initial appointment.

I often wonder what the locals make of this. This is a city where the mayor's salary is about $75,000 and where those earning the minimum wage ($5.15 per hour) struggle to rent a one-room apartment and pay the utility bills. In the zany world of intercollegiate athletics, the key to riches is not getting hired, but fired; it pays to foul up: Peter Principle perfection. According to a recent issue of the *Indiana Alumni Newsletter*, the biggest severance payment in recent years was given to a short-lived Director of Athletics, the very one on whose watch the executive suite was refurbished. This gentleman walked away from IU after less than two years on the job with a lump sum of more than $800,000. Money hemorrhages from IU's Athletics Department to pay off out-of-favor administrators and gaggles of fired coaches. We've had four or five football coaches since I showed up here, and we still can't kick our way out of a paper bag and into one of those bowls. There was the ill-fated Mr. Dinardo who amassed quite a losing record (nothing unusual there) during his three years as football coach. But that didn't seem to matter when the time came to sever our ties. This big-time loser reportedly departed with his $225,000 salary (for two years) plus the cash value of his contract buyout. The roughly $1 million IU will pay Dinardo to stay away is money down the drain: lifetime employment for about three of the university's lower paid, loyal staff, to be precise.

I'm no accountant, but if we just stuck with one (losing) coach instead of hiring and firing several (losing) coaches and giving each of them fistfuls of dollars to go away having failed to do what we paid them to do in the first place, we'd at least be better off financially. I have never been to the aforementioned refurbished executive suite, but I wouldn't be in the least bit surprised to find a framed version of this Groucho Marx quote on the wall: "What's a thousand dollars? Mere chicken feed. A poultry matter."

As if to underscore my general point, the university today announced the departure of Coach Davis. Speculation had been rife for some time that IU's basketball supremo might be less than secure in his job, but no doubt it took the lawyers some time to finesse the terms and conditions of the $800,000 severance package. Would that the rest of us could be relieved of our duties thus featherbedded. Try telling the Townies that we don't live in an ivory tower.

# SEX CYMBAL

MOVIE STUDIOS LUST AFTER OSCARS; UNIVERSITIES covet Nobel prizes. Cambridge University's website proclaims with justifiable pride that 80 affiliates have won the Big Gong since 1904, some 31 going to fabled Trinity College alone.

Indiana University is necessarily, and wisely, modest about its accomplishments in this regard. The good news is that James Watson received his Ph.D. from IU in 1950, before going on to win the 1962 Nobel Prize in Physiology or Medicine with Francis Crick. Thanks to them, DNA is part of every high schooler's ABC. Watson worked in the top floor of (still standing and much renovated) Kirkwood Hall with two other future laureates, Salvador Luria and Renato Dulbecco. What heady times those must have been. The bad news is that the phones have not been ringing of late to invite current IU faculty to Stockholm. The halcyon days are long gone.

But all is not lost. This is Bloomington, remember; the tiny town that splattered sex all over the map of modern America; where Alfred C. Kinsey catalogued gall wasps before stinging a nation into belated sexual awareness. It's a brand manager's dream come true.

Think Bloomington, think Kinsey; think Kinsey, think sex; think sex, think Hollywood; think Hollywood, think…six foot four Liam Neeson. The erstwhile boxing boyo from Ballymena did himself proud. More importantly, he did Kinsey justice. And he put camera-shy Bloomington back in the limelight, whether we like it or not. Kinsey, of course, would have dismissed such shenanigans. Once when asked about the idea of a movie being made on his life, he replied: "I can't think of anything more pointless."

Bill Condon's (imagine if the second "n" had been entered as "m" on his birth certificate by a hung-over registry clerk) movie about the life and times of Bloomington's most (in)famous professor is based on Jonathan Gathorne-Hardy's even-handed biography, *Kinsey*. The biopic was shot on location on the east coast (Columbia and Fordham universities), though you'd never guess, as one collegiate Gothic building is pretty much like any other. Laura Linney co-stars in the role of Mac, Kinsey's long-suffering wife. There was a special pre-release presentation in Bloomington: tickets were $20; movie plus cocktails was $50; movie plus reception and the chance to hobnob with Condon and Linney a mere $1,000. Proceeds went to the Institute named after him. *Kinsey* captures the monomania, humanity and psychological complexity of a man whose name is still enough to bring placard-waving Christian conservatives onto the steps of the local courthouse on a Saturday afternoon. The dispiriting marriage of family values and junk science at the anti-Kinsey altar reminds us daily that this country's Puritan roots are as deep and strong as ever. It's as if the world has stood still for half a century, despite the starred scientist's Herculean efforts to open the American mind.

Kinsey's redbrick, two-story home on First Street is a stone's throw from my present abode. It has a certain Hansel and Gretel-ish aspect to it, but I've yet to see perverts with pocket cameras skulking around the garden trying to snap the attic room where the Diabolic One recorded *those* films of locals in *flagrante delicto*. Participant observation is one thing, but priapic participation—even in the cause of science! The antics of Kinsey and his fornicating entourage have been a source of endless speculation for decades. Who did what with whom?

The number of people alive who may know "the facts" is tiny and dwindling daily: Kinsey died 50 years ago. Scholars will naturally continue to weigh in, but the Kinsey Institute for Research in Sex, Gender, and Reproduction, itself, opts for a hands-off approach—judicious or lilly livered depending on your viewpoint. The Institute's website has a list of frequently asked questions, the first of which has to do with this most delicate of issues: "We don't know everything about the intimacies of Alfred Kinsey's life (we leave that to the biographers), but we do know that he and his staff wanted to understand the variety of human sexual behavior." So far so good. On the specifics of who copulated with whom in the home movies depicting sexual activity, the Institute notes demurely that there "were only a few of these films made, and those were of selected staff and spouses, as well as a handful of volunteers." And with that, the FAQ moves on to other less tricky topics.

In retrospect, it is almost beyond belief that Kinsey could have flowered in this desert of illiberalism. We learn from a *Kinsey* footnote that it was an offence to "incite or encourage masturbation" in the state of Indiana, yet in this unsophisticated college town, the most sophisticated analyses ever of human sexual behavior would be conducted. But not even the indefatigable Kinsey and his devoted acolytes could have brought forth their two seismic volumes on male and female human sexuality without the protection of the jovially gifted Herman B Wells, whose unwavering commitment to the principle of academic freedom, in the flesh and the abstract, ensured the viability of Kinsey's enterprise and set the gold standard for future defenses of intellectual freedom in American higher education.

Despite the passing of 50 years and the sexual revolution of the Swinging Sixties, the axes are still out for Kinsey and anything to do with the man or his legacy, which makes directing the eponymous institute something of a challenge. The Kinsey Institute has had its critics over the years, both intra- and extra-murally, and, as a consequence, does not exactly go out of its way to attract media attention. You can't just walk into the Institute as you can into the Wells Library or any of IU's other academic buildings. Tours of its premises and collections take place at standard times or by appointment. I took the tour once and found it most informative and quite inoffensive: there was scarcely a titter or flush of color from any of the visitors. The Institute (which has moved from building to building in the course of its checkered history) houses a wealth of objects and art works that are regrettably little known. It's not hard to see why Gathorne-Hardy talked about the "acute paranoia" that haunts the Kinsey as being like "the afterglow of the Big Bang."

But it's not just the locals who get hot under the collar when it comes to Kinsey and the subject whereof we cannot speak. Letters poured into the editor of the *Indiana Alumni Magazine* at the end of 2004 to express outrage at the words "Sex, Sex and More Sex" having been splashed across the cover of the previous issue. From Baton Rouge: "Your recent cover was in extremely bad taste and continues to exhibit the liberal attitude that has permeated IU." Closer to home: "Once again I'm embarrassed for my alma mater…I have a freshman at Bloomington this year and was reluctant to send her, fearing exactly this type of attitude." These are the voices of IU graduates, not the Taliban. Fifty years on and the self-righteousness that Kinsey confronted on almost all sides shows no sign of abating.

Kinsey's mania for collecting, whether gall wasps, personal sex histories, or erotic art, has stood IU and the wider community in good stead. Blushing Bloomington is now home to one of the world's premier collections of publications, artifacts and information relating to human sexuality and its representation. The Institute routinely mounts public exhibitions such as "Eroticism and Music," "Sex and Humor," "The Power of Seduction," "The Kiss," or "The Art of Desire." How many other public (or private) universities can match that achievement? More to the point, how many would dare? If there were a Nobel Prize for academic leadership, Herman B Wells would surely be *primus inter pares* for posthumous consideration.

# RUSH HOUR

THIS VIGNETTE IS NEITHER ABOUT HELLISH traffic nor being in a state of Limbaugh. It's an altogether different kind of rush, one that was entirely Greek to me until I came to Bloomington. But let me let the newspapers do the explaining. The first headline is from the Sunday issue of the *Herald-Times:* "Grueling greek tradition draws hundreds." Despite what you may think, this has about as much to do with running a marathon as Pheidippides had to do with the invention of *Scrabble*. The second headline is courtesy of the *IDS*: "Tears, joy mark end of IU women's rush." This equally cryptic headline refers to a Greek tragedy, just not the sort with which most of us are familiar. I can do no better than quote one of the tragedians in question: "Me and my best friend got in. I'm so happy, we're both crying." Not quite an heroic hexameter, but…

One would be forgiven for thinking that these are the words of an airhead who has just auditioned successfully for a reality TV program. Nothing of the sort. This is an IU undergraduate expressing her feelings on having been invited to join the sorority of her choice. Back to the *IDS's* hyperventilating, preposition-challenged story:

"Sunday morning freshman Leslie Jobb had nothing left to do but wait. She made it through 19-, 12-, six- and three-party with only a few minor disappointments and sleepless nights. However she was in love with one sorority, and by 1 p.m. she would find out if the sisters there felt the same." Well, she did, and they did. Or, in the parlance of this pixilated sub-culture, "she got a bid."

Bloomington is home to almost fifty Greek-letter organizations (sororities and fraternities), a tradition that goes back, locally, one hundred and fifty years. Yet, in the middle of the winter, in the mid-West, in the twenty first century, hundreds of almost identically dressed girls stand in agitated huddles across from Alpha this, Delta that and Omega the other sororities ("chapters," as they're known) waiting to discover if their infantile dreams will come true. Here's how the paper captured the moment for one nervous wreck: "As a little girl, Shannon Lee dreamed of being a princess and being a member of a sorority. A knock on her third-floor dorm today will decide whether her childhood sorority fantasy comes true." Shannon, by the way, is a "self-proclaimed 'pink girl'" who chose "a rose-colored chiffon pink dress with matching strappy sandals that wrap around the ankles as her final outfit." Just the ticket, I thought, as I eyed the thermometer needle twitching around the 28 degree mark. These kids ain't any old Greeks; they're Spartans. And they sure as hell need to be since this rushing business ("recruitment" in sorority speak) can also be an ego-bruising experience for the less than preppily perfect. Once again, the local paper: "The whole rush process can make some girls seem insecure and promote feelings of inadequacy—not pretty enough, not thin enough, not smart enough."

Nobody will admit it openly, but looks matter mightily in the rushing business. The "rushees," aping the "sisters," are dressed, painted and coiffed just so, as if following a tacitly known formula.

Not so much as a standard deviation. The nation's orthodontists, tanning salons and hair colorists have done their job. A plentitude of plastic pulchritude is on parade. Proof positive comes in the form of the display ads that some sororities run in the *IDS* to congratulate their new members. You'll find no black sheep in these photogenic flocks: unnerving perfection salutes the unsuspecting reader. One Ms. Nicolini was quoted as saying, "It's all a vibe. You hit it off or you don't." Well, maybe. But if you look like the back of a bus, you've as much chance of recording a vibe as you do of witnessing a tsunami in Lake Monroe. These latter day Helens of Troy fuse narcissism and superficiality in a way that makes Sebastian Flyte's Oxonian sybaritism seem downright amateurish. And if you're a drop-dead gorgeous lesbian, it's probably better not to come out until you are safely inside. The issue of sexual orientation is still not one with which the Greek system seems altogether comfortable.

But perhaps I'm being uncharitable. Omear Khalid, a vice-president of the IU Interfraternity Council, would presumably agree. "People only hear about deaths," the VP announced to the *IDS* before adding that "we need to get away from this theory that there is a divide between greeks and non-greeks and create a better campus environment." As a non-greek—though I must confess that I had never actually thought of myself in that way before—I could only concur. But that was before I'd logged onto the IU Panhellenic Association's Web site. After reading the "19 Reasons to go Greek" I quickly realized that my non-greek status was a boon in disguise. Apparently, one would "go greek" for reasons such as IU Sing (#6), Parents (sic) Weekend (#11), Dance Marathon (#14) and Chapter Pride (#18). Frankly, I think I'd recommend a full-frontal lobotomy instead, with or without anesthesia.

# BLOOMINGTON'S BODY MASS

Ranking is a national pastime: there are published rankings for everything under the sun, from symphony orchestras to liberal arts colleges. And, of late, obesity. Indiana has just been ranked the tenth fattest state in nation by the American Obesity Association; Mississippi, however, takes the biscuit (lots of it). According to another set of rankings, Indianapolis shed a few pounds between 2003 and 2004 to move gracefully from 12th to 17th position in the lard stakes. First time visitors to the U.S. cannot but be struck by the rising tide of flab as one travels to the interior from either coast: the slice of humanity one sees when departing San Diego airport is much thinner than that waiting at Indianapolis. Kilometers inward translate into kilos on board. In the words of another *emigré*—journalist Andrew Sullivan—America has become a nation of "lardaceous couch potatoes, stuffed silly with saturated victimhood," lounging, he might have added, in their leather La-Z-boys.

Bloomington is bi-modal when it comes to corpulence. There are featherweights and heavyweights; Kate Moss look-alikes and lumbering three hundred pounders. How, I often ask myself, does the former metamorphose into the latter? Iron buns and sacks of cellulite may share the same physical space, but they surely don't inhabit the same calorific universe. What turns Adonis into adipose?

As you might expect, these are not subjects that can be discussed lightly. Try calling someone "fat" on campus and the collective gasp of horror will be audible in Illinois. The more manifestly fat the nation becomes, the less acceptable it is to call a fat spade a fat spade. The literal weight of evidence counts for naught. I take my hat off to Greg Critser for publishing *Fat Land*, a no-folds-barred insight into the history of American obesity. These days being fat is: (a) someone else's fault; (b) something that just happens to you; (c) an illness; (d) a function of socio-economic disadvantage. I remember wandering the shabby streets of Addis Ababa and not noticing much evidence of obesity.

Fifteen-year old Gregory Rhymes, who weighs in at 400 lbs, likes to "super-size" his orders at McDonald's. Apparently he sees no connection between his eating habits and his BMI (Body Mass Index) and so proceeds to sue the company because their burgers made him fat. "It wasn't me, guv, honest." Nothing new there. You develop emphysema, so you take the tobacco company to court in pursuit of a seven-figure settlement. Never mind the fact that the words of the Surgeon General are emblazoned across the pack and that anyone who's got an anorexic pea for a brain knows that smoking is probably not the best way to ensure longevity.

Litigants are showing great imagination. A disgruntled 350-lb female driver tried—unsuccessfully—to make Honda provide her with a seat belt extender for her Odyssey. And if I were a betting man, I'd wager that a class action lawsuit is imminent against Southwest Airlines, which makes customers who cannot fit in the regular airline seat pay for two. What is so astonishing is that lawsuits, which most rational folks would deem frivolous, are filed in delusional sincerity by the offended parties. For the record, the claim filed against McDonald's was dismissed by the sitting judge with the sage words: "Nobody is forced to eat at McDonald's."

As I watch 12-inch pizzas being washed down with giant-sized Cokes by locals who can scarcely haul their drooping *derrières* out of their sagging suburbans and as I sit in the cinema listening to fistfuls of popcorn being scooped mindlessly from jumbo-sized buckets into cavernous Hoosier maws, what little sympathy I might have had for my fellow man evaporates. Here, as elsewhere in Middle America, the reasons for fatness are inescapably obvious: laziness and greed. We live in a post-ambulatory, drive-in-through-and-out society, where eating is an end-in-itself. We don't need sophisticated behavioral research and epidemiological analysis to tell us what we already know. Obesity is largely self-inflicted.

Even more perplexing, these heavyweights are not just unfazed by their BMI but blissfully immune to social embarrassment. They seem to take comfort from the fact that others of comparable girth are everywhere to be seen. If half the population is overweight, then being overweight is normal. So, it is the broccoli-chomping ectomorphs who are the deviants. But there is hope. The local press profiled an IU student who shed a spectacular 100 lbs. to go from a size 28—is there such?—to a size 4. She did it without pills or a gastric bypass. In short, she chose to loose weight. She persisted. Finally, she succeeded. Said Susan Eley: "I was tired of feeling listless and sitting on the couch every night." Couch potatoes of Bloomington take note.

But Bloomington is more than Lardsville, IN. Here beer bellies, triple chins and love handles co-exist with rippling six packs and pert pecs. Lately, parts of gentrified downtown Bloomington are aglow at night, gym-front windows packed with body-conscious students toning up muscles the *Lumpenproletariat* never even knew it had. Nowhere, perhaps, is the contrast between (senior) town and (junior) gown so poignantly, so cruelly exhibited.

# VILLAGE LIFE

IT TOOK ME A WHILE TO take the measure of Bloomington, but once I'd done my homework I knew there was only one place to live: the faculty ghetto. Longtime residents of the neighborhood refer to it, sometimes a mite self-consciously, as Elm Heights. Those on the fringes or, perish the thought, technically beyond the pale, seem to experience the same kind of social anxiety that's associated with securing certain cachet-charged LA area phone numbers or London postal codes. But the ghetto, with its fetching jumble of architectural genres (Federal, Greek Revival, Queen Anne, Colonial Revival, Four-Square and much else), mature trees and warmly inviting character, has the look and feel of a naturally evolved neighborhood, where people stroll, children play and easy exchanges take place. Elm Heights is at once a million miles and a mere mile from the rash of soulless developments and archly named sub-divisions (e.g., Hyde Park, Kensington) that embody the contemporary Bloomington version of the American domiciliary dream.

A brisk five-minute walk along some of the city's finest residential streets and through the best of IU's well tended, neo-

Gothic buildings and you're in the heart of the sprawling campus. No traffic, no hassle. There is, of course, a price to pay. The better houses are often sold privately or so quickly that dithering, surveying and haggling are simply out of the question. Within a 200-yard radius of our abode there lived professors of chemistry, mathematics, history, classics, biology, comparative literature, law, philosophy and who knows what else. You couldn't swing a cat without bruising a brainiac. It was hard not to develop an inferiority complex. There was enough high-grade grey matter within a square mile of our Foursquare to create a mini university.

But old houses demand tender, loving care. Especially in Elm Heights. Which brings us to the subject of—if I may be permitted an anachronism or two—craftsmen, handymen and tradesmen: the boon and bane of one's quotidian life in Bloomington. They come in three varieties: (1) the praeternaturally decent professional, (2) the occasionally bumbling but just about forgivable rascal, and (3) the unreconstructed chancer. I'm on my fourth home in Bloomington and I've had more walls painted, floors installed, carpets laid, roofs repaired, doors unhinged, lavatories unbunged than an entire series of *Changing Rooms*. Carpenters, plumbers, roofers and glaziers move in and out of my world as frequently as illegal immigrants cross the Tex-Mex border.

Over the years I have developed a sixth sense that swiftly picks out the chancer. You can see the syllogism forming in their heads: *If* this dork lives in Elm Heights *and* speaks with a weird British accent, *then* quadruple the regular quote. I was once given two estimates for removing a sixty-foot tree: one was in excess of $2,000, the other $500. At the end of the proverbial day the tree would be gone, whichever arboreal expert perpetrated the deed, so I was puzzled as to what I would get for the additional $1,500. Answer:

a lot of eco-friendly mumbo-jumbo and tree-hugging sentimentality. The sycamore bit the dust and nary a tear was shed.

We heads-in-the-clouds Gownies are considered fair game by some of the Townies who earn their daily bread by the sweat of their brow. Don't get me wrong: I respect (envy, to tell the truth) the skills I see exhibited by craftsmen proudly plying their trade and feel woefully inadequate each time I call on the services of our favorite ice-fishing-in-Montana handyman, himself an unsurpassable storehouse of parochial gossip, to do what any self-respecting male, let alone one with a sack full of degrees to his name, should be able to do. In my defense I can only point out that Bertrand Russell, if he is to be believed, couldn't boil a kettle of water to make himself a cup of tea. I believe it's called trained incapacity. I'm very well trained in that department.

And then there are those whose desperate desire to succeed can create an initially false impression. We had our driveway black-topped between downpours of tropical intensity by a young man and his wife for a measly $100. If he topped us and our immediate neighbors, then, perhaps, he could exercise a monopoly on the street and generate repeat business, seemed to be his reasoning. One could not but admire his determination and feel shamefaced at both underpaying and underestimating him (I had initially slotted him into the cozener category).

My first house painter not only overcharged me but also behaved rather truculently. I was pleased to see the back of his brush. But I remember his successor with affection. He came in under his original, highly reasonable estimate. His workmanship was impeccable, his manners likewise. I don't think he was guilty of hubris by calling his business "The Painter;" at least he didn't italicize the definite article. He was one of those gems whose reputation was established through the village's social circuitry; not for him flash advertising and loud claims in the *Yellow Pages*. He was so highly regarded that it was a struggle to get his name: reputation is a hushed asset in these parts.

When it comes to cars, I make Bertrand Russell seem like a beginner in the trained incapacity stakes. I'm still not sure whether the engine lies under the hood or trunk; words, you understand, that have no automotive connotations in the U.K. But after the inevitable exposure to some slippery grease monkeys, I found my man. Worldwide Motors is a textbook case of what micro-entrepreneurship is all about. Don, the owner-manager, taught math before moving under the hoods of Bloomington's disproportionately large population of German, Swedish and Japanese imports. This guy knows his onions and my big end like no other mechanic I've ever met. Even when he shifts into lay speak, I still feel like a cretin. But what the hell, he's smart, professional and trustworthy. He walks all the marketing talk about personalization, customer care and community engagement. So does the sparkling Mary who runs the front of the shop with aplomb. It's almost a pleasure to see the smoke billowing forth from under the hood knowing that I'll soon be on the receiving end of premium service delivered with a high wattage smile.

But for every Don, there's a nameless plumber, fitter or lawn carer who seems not to understand that in a village word gets about. Cut your margins, but certainly not corners, if you want to succeed long term, is my advice to these rapscallions, for the conductivity of Bloomington's gossip networks is second to none. Much in the realm of repairs, refurbishment and renovation depends on word-of-mouth referral. It's not like Peru or other parts of the developing world where half the population belongs to the "black" economy. Here, almost everything is white and above board. Moreover, there is considerable evidence of what e-commerce pundits like to call "swift trust." The Townies are often inherently reliable; their handshake, their word is their bond. The trouble is that their other word is all too often *mañana*. Jobs begin with an encouraging burst of energy and enthusiasm, but then things start to stall. The hired hands disappear. Days, weeks can go by before even simple tasks are completed. No malice is intended; it's not personal, just the Hoosier way.

In Bloomington there's no hiding: everyone is just two steps away from everyone else. I learned this basic fact of Bloomington life at Mirá, *the* salon for those in the know. It was established—then successfully sold—by Claire, a spirited English lassie, who probably would have been an architect if she hadn't got into the tonsorial business. One minute she's trimming my locks, the next she's removing a colleague's split ends or retouching the roots of my sworn enemy. What a parade of personalities in this hot house of snipping and sniping. What a source of community intelligence Pendlebury's Hair Studio is! I never leave without thinking of William Congreve: "I know that's a secret, for it's whispered every where."

# BLATHERING IN THE BLOGOSPHERE

To blog is to be. Blogging is CB radio on steroids. These days Hyde Park Corner is only a few HTML tags away. The Web has become the universal soapbox. No voice need be unheard; no whine denied oxygen. It's the fusion of vanity publishing and the bully pulpit. Every idea, no matter how trite or crazy, can see the light of digital day. Blowhards, from Boston to Bloomington, are working their knitted socks off. There are terabytes of trivia sloshing around in the blogosphere, 99% of it unread and unreadable. There are almost as many windbags as potential readers, maybe more. It makes for a seriously skewed distribution (a power law in statistical speak). A few blogs attract most of the eyeballs; most blogs are ignored.

However, in my gleeful disparaging of this Web epiphenomenon, I seriously underestimated its journalistic significance. Trent Lott and Dan Rather did as well; and lost their jobs. At least that is what the blogging community would have us believe. Blogs can keep stories alive, bring them to the surface and propel them into the media mainstream. *Nota bene*: a new communicative dynamic is at work in the public sphere.

Researchers like to categorize blogs as being personal or themed, individualistic or communitarian in character. Some blogs are like pamphlets or broadsheets, others more like diaries or journals. Many genres and sub-genres can be identified. An example of the topical blog is *Indiana Students for the Digital Commons,* an interactive site that aims to provide information and links on developments and issues relating to the scholarly/digital commons. This is a group blog with a clear informational/educational focus. There are also coteries of blogging students who interact routinely and intensively with one another on study-related matters—an example of the communicative kind.

Personal bloggers—reflecting the geekiness of this sub-culture—go in for silly, if harmless, names and titles. *Sampo, the Journal of Abundant Media*; *popou's Journal*; *Metajaleh*; *Thus Spake the Princess*; *Professional-Lurker*; *Geek-guides.com*. To be fair, their blogs have some redeeming features, but often it's sophomoric, stream of consciousness stuff. The *Princess* posts this unfiltered revelation at 12.53: "i'm watching craig ferguson now and then i think i am off to bed. i need some good zzz's. nighty night." Who, I wondered, would be interested in knowing this? More to the point, why would anyone post such a banality? Why is a tissue of throwaway, domestic conversation being projected into the public sphere?

Metajaleh begins: "Well, I know I haven't posted in a while. Mostly that is due to having not a lot to say…Man, I have a lot of shit to do…the rest of my life is pretty boring." In which case why bother blogging? Why, dear Metajaleh, inflict such narcissistic ramblings on the world-at-large? What desperate craving for attention is indicated by this kind of online outpouring? One writes a diary for one's personal satisfaction; it is a private act, though in exceptional cases these personal chronicles may be published because of their literary, cultural or historical merit.

poupou (note the pretentious lower case *p*) takes us to another level. "Chris, my boyfriend of almost two years, has decided that what he wants is to remain in the small town where we got our degrees…He needs to think about his life and what he wants to do next, he says. So every day I wake up to the person I love and spend the rest of the day watching the clock, waiting for the moment that our relationship ends." I don't know poupou and I don't know Chris from Adam, yet I now know more about their personal lives that I either want to know or should know. In society we have filters that curtain off the intimate and personal from the shared and the public, but discretion is *passé* in an age of confessional excess. Who really cares about poupou and Chris? For whom is she writing? Why is she exposing her unremarkable and unedifying private life to strangers? What prompts this particular kind of digital exhibitionism? What makes such behavior socially acceptable in cyberspace?

Sampo tells us that he's begun yoga classes and that he has long been a fan of Ghandi, concluding his post with the profound: "I sound like a total shithead, and for my next post, the 'Pete's a Flake' rating will shoot further skyward." You may say that this is just harmless thinking out loud. Out loud, it may be (in a manner of speaking) but thinking it is not. Rather it is a bathetic form of self-presentation—performance, if you prefer—favored, it seems, by those not always entirely comfortable in the real world and blessed with less than optimally developed social and linguistic skills: *vide* the self-conscious use of slang and expletives.

I trawled around for some Bloomington blogs. *Star Shaped* (*The musings and life of a 23 year old woman living in the midwestern United States*) opened with the memorable "Blah, blah, blah…I'm listening to Blur, drinking Diet Coke, and just in general bumming around…" In an earlier post, *Star Shaped* tells us that she "tried on a wedding dress…complete with veil and tiara," adding, much, no doubt, to the relief of her future spouse, that she's "officially much more excited about (her) wedding day, which is less than four months away." Even the Townies are electronic egotists.

*Scheiss Weekly* manages to match this level of vacuity: "I LOVE candles. When did I stop burning them? This must begin again, immediately." On *Sallad's Blog* I learn that she attended her "second Weight Watchers meeting today and was pleasantly surprised that (she) had lost 3.8 lbs." We are then given an overview of her dietary practices and told that her "weakness time is 3–6PM." Who on earth cares? In any case, 3.8 lbs in the massively obese Hoosier state is a drop in the cellulite bucket.

*Just Watch the Fireworks* provides a merciful break from the mundane monologues, offering instead a series of recommendations about what to watch, read and listen to. We are not, of course, told why one should heed *Just Watch the Fireworks'* recommendations. Like so many bloggers, this fellow simply believes that his views warrant the world's attention. Perhaps we shouldn't be surprised. Blogging is the great equalizer; my voice matters as much as yours, and to hell with cognitive authority, cultural acuity, editorial oversight and integrity checking. All opinions are equal in the blogging barnyard.

Why can't these good souls decouple from their computers, leave their offices and living rooms and try talking to one another face-to-face? Their digital dribblings are, after all, the stuff of everyday conversation: the sort of stuff that was meant to be heard, but certainly not seen or read. As they might say, though not, perish the thought, of themselves: "Get a life!"

# COMMUNITY SPIRIT

SCRUFFY STUDENTS AND A SCUFFED BUILDING reeking of stale beer. That's a typical students' union in a British university. Things are different here. The Indiana Memorial Union (or IMU as its universally and affectionately known) is neither scuffed nor scruffy, just a little tired. This leviathan sits slap bang in the heart of the campus and bears as much resemblance to a British union as a whale does to a whelk. First off, the IMU's footprint and presence are massive: 500,000 square feet of space and a formidable tower that rises proudly over the campus. This is no ordinary union.

To be sure, you'll find students swotting in wood paneled workspaces, sleeping in Chesterfield couches, or arched, cue in hand, over rectangles of green baize, but the IMU is much more than a haunt for young minds. This, after all, is the self-described "campus centerpiece...home away from home, and gathering place." The IMU is a centripetal force to be reckoned with; it sucks faculty, students, alumni, visitors and locals into its orbit. There's a 186-bedroom hotel, a hairdressing saloon, numerous eateries and meeting rooms, a bookstore and much else woven into the fabric of the building.

First time visitors will be puzzled by the lack of clear demarcation lines. They may also be puzzled by the incongruous presence of a gleaming, full-sized Venus de Milo in the foyer, though relieved that the prudish Hoosiers have not yet felt a need to cover her naughty bits. Hotel guests may well find themselves clambering over the prostrate bodies of napping students as, following check-in, they navigate the mezzanine floor en route to their room. One minute you're in the hotel zone the next you're in the general swirl. Turn right instead of left and you could find yourself at a fund-raising meeting or retirement party rather than your bedroom. I stayed in the IMU many moons ago and was flummoxed both by the unorthodoxy of the spatial arrangements and also the lack of a decent restaurant: the Tudor Room, with its high-ceilings, beams and mock regimental flags (each academic school has its own flag and colors for graduation), is fine for lunch but perversely closes its doors immediately thereafter: come nightfall and even a semi-serious diner has to head off-campus for a meal. And try getting a glass of wine or shot of whiskey in this place, day or night! I routinely warn visitors from Europe to come armed with a bottle or two of claret. A dry campus is one thing, but a dry hotel is commercial madness.

The IMU is a maze of passages, hidden stairways, nooks and crannies. University Chancellor Ken Gros Louis—the embodiment of Wellsian values—tells the story of how one afternoon the novelist Stanley Elkin called him saying that he was hopelessly lost in the Union and that he expected to see an ancient mariner-type figure who would tell him that he had been adrift in the building for 14 years. My son calls the IMU his second home without a scintilla of sarcasm; it's a favorite port of call for some of his high school chums when the lure of downtown fades. Rafael has wormed his way into parts of the building I didn't even know existed and has in the process found and test driven enough pianos—baby grands and uprights—to meet the needs of numerous orchestras. If the IMU should ever need an official guide, he's their man.

One minute you're surrounded by ghastly fast food outlets, the next you're staring at a 12-lane, 10-pin bowling alley. A bookstore that sells every conceivable kind of IU gift and branded apparel for every age and taste sits next to a study area warmed by a log fire. The Union is stuffed to the gills with plaques for distinguished servants of the university and major donors. Walls are bedecked with photographs of past presidents, notable alumni and distinguished faculty. Make a gift or make your mark and you'll not be forgotten. The IMU is also home to a motley collection of *objets d'art* and artifacts, ranging from copper lusterware and ancient oak trunks to a signed letter from France's World War I military hero, Marshal Ferdinand Foch: it's the Aladdin's cave of academe. Posh dinners take place in the Federal Room with it elegant anteroom and cabinets full of quirky antiques—well-meaning alumni and friends sometimes give the oddest things to Old IU. This is not quite high table at Balliol or King's, but it's a touching Hoosier nod in the right direction.

I have never seen a uniformed security guard at the IMU nor, come to think of it, anywhere in the university. This is an open campus, trusting and accessible to Townies as well as Gownies. Such a situation would be inconceivable in a British university, even a small one. Go to the basement of the IMU on a Sunday afternoon and you will find several of the bowling alleys and pool tables happily occupied by Bloomington families and teenagers. The IMU is theirs as much as ours. No one seems to question that university facilities should be open to the public. No one even seems to notice. Town and gown amuse themselves as one in this jolly giant of a building.

# THE FOUR SEASONS

THE ACADEMIC YEAR CULMINATES WITH COMMENCEMENT. That way it never ends. The cyclical rhythms of university life are enshrined in its calendar, ceremonials and symbols, captured beautifully by P. F. Kluge in his *Alma Mater: A College Homecoming*. In my undergraduate days, the three academic terms were routinely referred to as Michaelmas, Hillary and Trinity, anachronistic language associated with the ecclesiastical calendar of the Anglican Christian year. With the advent of the semester system and the demise of Latin, we have to make do with spring and fall semesters. Sadly, simplification comes at a price, but at least the seasonality of academic life persists.

I came to Bloomington from Glasgow, Scotland. There it rained, doggedly and spitefully, year-round. There may have been four seasons, but one would never have known. As Irvine Welsh, the nation's answer to Marcel Proust, put it: "Supposed tae be August, but ah'm fuckin freezing ma baws off here." Rain was an equal opportunity season spoiler; and like the poor, it was always with us.

Here, by way of contrast, the seasons are powerfully, magnificently differentiated, sometimes all in the same day.

Hoosiers quickly learn which Vivaldi track Nature is playing: the seasonal spectrum ranges from sub-Artic winters (it's fifteen degrees below zero as I write and coruscating snow is piled seventeen inches high) to monsoon-like thunderstorms during the torrid summers: if we're really lucky, the odd twister will stray a few degrees from Tornado Alley and send us scampering to our basements. The mercury in our therometer moves as if on performance enhancing drugs, careering from minus Heaven-knows-what to almost 100. Don't take my word for it, take S. J. Perlman's: "The weather is always capricious in the Middle West, and although it was midsummer, the worst blizzard in Chicago's history greeted us on arrival." North Dakotan winters and Arizonian summers may put Indiana in the shade, but, for those of us from temperate climes, this is something else; stereophonic, synesthetic *Donner und Blitzen*. We aliens are gobsmacked by the grandeur of it all.

The panzer-like assault by V8-powered SUVs on Bloomington in late August is saluted by glorious, azure skies and crystalline light worthy of the Mediterranean. It's the perfect climatic complement to the trim, tanned bodies that tumble forth from Detroit's finest. Freshmen, ears glued to their cell phones, shriek and flap, as sweat-smudged parents haul the latest in white goods and digital paraphernalia from pantechnicons to elevated dorms, stepping stones for the lucky ones to the Greek house of their provincial dreams.

Sublime September announces the slow drift into the russet and saffron of the Hoosier fall, the raw material of T. C. Steele's painterly imagination. Steele, patriarch of Indiana impressionists, was the man who put nearby Brown County on the map and on countless canvases—not a few of which are to be found on the walls of the IMU. The local palette may not quite match New England, but it's enough to draw caravans from Chicago to Little Nashville and the enveloping Hoosier National Forest. Foreign students, in particular, seem mesmerized by the leafy spectacle afforded by Indiana in the autumn.

Come November, the Chancellor's witty welcome is long forgotten. Freshmen, no longer grappling with upside-down city maps, now have hooded sweatshirts and the overcompensating swagger of the still not wholly self-assured. Rites of passage have been negotiated or circumnavigated. Newness is fading along with summer tans. Term papers are displacing re-runs of *Friends* and hours of *Trivial Pursuit*, as the nights draw in and academic deadlines draw near. Come Thanksgiving, we're almost on the final stretch. The weeklong exodus is dramatic; Bloomington seems like a giant, deserted opera set. Then back they all come to the pressures of exam week and final grades before heading home again for Kwanzaa.

Christmas in Bloomington is often picture postcard perfect, but postcards don't convey the bone marrow-chilling cold of a serious Indiana winter. If you're from Thailand or Tonga, fresh snow for the first time is irresistible. But snow is not radioactive nuclear waste, for which a detailed handling guide is needed, despite what one precious administrator seems to think: "A special message to those graduate students who have not experienced snow before: Take a walk through campus; it's magical! Build a snowman! Stay warm! For those of you tempted to drive your cars: don't! It's better to take the bus or to walk. Driving in these conditions can be very dangerous if you've never driven in snow before. And even if you know what you're doing, others may not." Talk about infantalization!

Gray pallor and grim skies, enlivened only by basket-balling passions, slowly cede to the cantankerous squalls that herald spring.

Founders Day in March brings a brief burst of brilliance, as peacock-like in our elegant robes we process and recess in honor of those who sowed the seeds back in 1820. The University has come a long way since its humble beginnings as a nominal seminary; at this time of year we hope the same can be said of the local hardwood heroes. "March madness" is a much-desired affliction in these parts. If the Hoosiers don't make it to the NCAA Final Sixteen, Prozac sales skyrocket across the state, which means that Indy-based Eli Lilly, manufacturer and patent holder of the happiness drug, is laughing all the way to the bank.

With the Floridian excesses of Spring Break now digitally memorialized and casually shared on *Flickr*, it's heads-down time. As the end of the academic year hooves into sight and the last of the cherry blossom fades, it's easy to see why Thomas Gaines anointed IU one of America's five most beautiful universities in his book, *The Campus as a Work of Art*. Gurgling streams, dry-stone walls and green meadows all bathed in heart-warming sunshine provide the cruelest of distractions for those hunched over computers or chained to their library carrels. *Al fresco* teaching is a popular compromise, as the re-bronzing season kicks into high gear.

The beginning of the end is also the end of the beginning. Those who hurl mortarboards and colored balloons skywards to the accompaniment of triumphal music in Memorial Stadium are beginning the next stage of their lives, symbolized by the moving of tassels from right side to left. It's now time to reload the rumbling SUVs and creaking Toyotas and bid *adios* to Old IU. For the rest, it's merely *hasta pronto*. Before long the panzer divisions will re-converge on Bloomington and all will be as it was. And ever will be.

# TUNES FOR TOWNS

"HIGH CHURCH, LOW STEEPLE, DIRTY STREETS, proud people."
Not my words and most certainly not words about Bloomington, but
Jonathan Swift expatiating on my birthplace, Newry, one of the oldest
and least regarded towns in Ireland. Its antiquity and former glory,
though well enough documented, are damnably difficult to discern,
even for the charitably inclined. There's no gainsaying a friend who
once described it, without malice, as the armpit of Ulster.

Post-war Newry had vestigial elements of *Angela's Ashes*:
slum dwellings, black-shawled crones, dingy lanes, gas lamps, silver-
topped milk bottles. I remember the drab fifties without fondness
and our modest attempts to swing in the sixties with nothing but
embarrassment. With the seventies came the nation's hardest-working
euphemism, The Troubles. I can still see the tracer bullets streaking
across the town's slate rooftops, feel the thudding explosions and
hear the sneering squaddies. The town went from bad to worse.

I'll confess to some *nostalgie de la boue*, but returning to
the torpid Clanrye river, mean houses and shuttered shops rapidly
removes any rose tint that the unflagging drizzle hasn't already begun

to wash away. My gut clenches when I espy the Bearnish and Slieve Gullion, westerly guardians of the Yew Tree at the Head of the Strand (which is what Newry means in the original Gaelic). The dirty streets that Swift immortalized are still there. As for the local pride, hubristically encapsulated in the city fathers' rebranding of their town as the Venice of the North—La Serenissima must be quaking in her watery boots—it's better described as parochial self-congratulation, the kind one associates with Belfast, Glasgow and post-9/11 New York.

I have tried to get close to my alma armpit, but it's difficult. It's not that the town hasn't done its bit: twenty years ago I was invited to open the spanking new public library, an event commemorated by a brass plaque somewhere on the first floor. There's a plangent song by Phil Coulter, *The Town I Loved So Well*, which can just about move the most cynical Celt to tears. It's not about Newry, but the Derry of The Troubles. Yet it could so easily have been written about the Newry of my childhood: it rings true, achingly so. Maybe if it had been, I could have forgiven the town that never smiled.

There are towns and cities one just falls head over heels in love with. Paris has more lovers than a New York tenement has roaches. Her charms are legendary. So, too, the songs about those perennial charms. Remember Cole Porter's *I Love Paris in the Springtime* or Vernon Duke's *April in Paris*? Of course, Paris doesn't have a monopoly on urban seduction. Frank Sinatra stirs the loins when he pounds out *New York, New York*. And San Francisco, that grabber of hearts, is not to be overlooked, especially when Tony Bennett is massaging the microphone. So few words, so much *genius loci*.

My one true love is London: I lived there for a decade and will always consider it home. Thomas de Quincey must have been consuming too much of the titular product when he wrote in

*Confessions of an English Opium Eater*: "A duller spectacle this earth of ours has not to show than a rainy Sunday in London." A few dog days in Bloomington's high summer would have opened his eyes. London is one of a kind: cultivated and cosmopolitan. And, I have to say, loutish and lewd. Quite apart from Handel's twelve *London* symphonies, the city on the Thames has had a slew of pop classics penned in her honor: think of Ralf McTell's haunting *Streets of London*—even if inspired by Paris. But great tunes are not the preserve of great capitals. *One More Sunday in Savannah*, from the mouth of Nina Simone, is a captivating window on the Southern soul. I don't know if cities get the songs or symphonies they deserve, but there is, surely, some kind of correlation between metropolitan magic and musical legacy.

A Hoosier great is Hoagy Carmichael, much written and talked about. His *Stardust* is the most recorded song in history, and—residents of Savannah take note—he also penned *Georgia on my Mind*. Mr. Carmichael was a native of Indiana and remains, perhaps, Indiana University's best-known alumnus. (*Hoagy's Songs* is a bumper CD performed by the Bloomington POPS Orchestra.) When not stardusting, he wrote one of our local anthems, *Chimes of Indiana*. I have seen rows of grown men and women locked arm in arm—think mawkish renditions of *Auld Lang's Ayne*—singing *Hail to Old IU* at the close of the university commencement ceremony. So moved are we all by the moment, that the orthographic distortion necessary to sustain the internal rhyming ("Gloriana Frangipana") is conveniently overlooked. Who cares if it should be "Frangipani" when the Hoosier juices are in spate?

I have dumped Newry, never having loved her in the first instance. My heart, at various times, has toyed with capitals and second-tier cities. Only recently have I come to realize that I may, despite my occasionally blustery protestations to the contrary, have begun to fall under the slow, subtle spell of a mid-Western college town. Was Bloomington where the trail would finally end? The lyrics of P. J. Harvey's *Is That All There Is?* spring to mind.

What is it about this flat-chested, sub-metropolitan settlement that hooks us? We come here, as we dutifully inform one another, not planning to stay, but years, decades, on we seem as attached to the University as a wasp to the rim of a Coke bottle on an August afternoon. What's in the local water, in the air, that neutralizes our *Wanderlust*? What is it about Indiana University that allows us to, if not overcome, at least accommodate what Sigmund Freud termed "the narcissism of minor differences"? Somehow the notion of an academic community seems to work; somehow the ideal of a university, if not always attained, is plausibly and energetically aspired to for much of the time by most of the community. I remain astonished that such a venture in such a place could succeed to such an extent. Moreover, that the enterprise should tolerate one's public ruminations on these and other matters over the years is almost too good to be true: a confirmation, piffling to be sure, of its continuing commitment to the defining values of the academy. So, Bloomington, Indiana, it is.

## ABOUT THE AUTHOR

Blaise Cronin was born and raised in Ireland. Trinity College Dublin and the Queen's University of Belfast graciously granted him the degrees necessary to avoid working for a living. He came to Middle America via London (England) and Glasgow (Scotland). In one sense, he has never looked back; in another, he has never stopped looking back.

Printed in the United States
209561BV00001B/406-408/A